Desktop
Typographic

D1444912

Desktop
Typographics

John Negru

VAN NOSTRAND REINHOLD
_____ New York

Library of Congress Catalog Card Number 90-49702
ISBN 0-442-00179-7

Designed and typeset by John Negru

Printed in the United States of America

Van Nostrand Reinhold
115 Fifth Avenue
New York, New York 10003

Chapman and Hall
2-6 Boundary Row
London, SE1 8HN, England

Thomas Nelson Australia
102 Dodds Street
South Melbourne 3205
Victoria, Australia

Nelson Canada
1120 Birchmount Road
Scarborough, Ontario M1K 5G4, Canada

16 15 14 13 12 11 10 9 8 7 6 5 4 3 2 1

Library of Congress Cataloging in Publication Data

Negru, John,
    Desktop typographics / John Negru.
      p.   cm.
    Includes index.
    ISBN 0-442-00179-7
    1. Desktop publishing—Style manuals.   2. Printing, Practical—
    Layout—Data processing.
    I. Title.
    Z286.D47N44   1991
    686.2'2544—dc20   90-49702
                                                                  CIP

This book is dedicated to you.
Seek wisdom, work for peace, and honor the words
that make them real.

Contents

Preface . . . . *ix*

Before You Begin 1

1. Fonts: Your Basic Building Blocks 13

2. Managing Your Fonts 35

3. Editing Your Fonts 43

4. Font Effects 53

5. Kerning 59

6. Templates 65

7. Utilities 71

8. Formware 83

9. Phototypesetter Drivers 93

10. PostScript Interpreters 99

11. File Managers 107

12. Service Bureaus 111

Professional Associations 121

Periodicals 125

Books 133

Vendors 147

Typographic Industry Terms and
Conditions of Sale 179

Index 189

Preface

If you are reading this, chances are that desktop publishing has already changed your life forever.

You already know DTP gives you the power to communicate directly and economically with others in ways never before possible. But to take advantage of this remarkable opportunity, you are faced with the daunting responsibility of learning something entirely new in order to do it right.

Publishing effectively involves many skills. Not all of these skills have changed with the desktop revolution, but typesetting is one that certainly has. *Desktop Typographics* is your pathfinder to the new world of typesetting in the electronic publishing environment.

Herein you will discover a complete, straightforward, and painstakingly researched guide to the processes, the products, and the pitfalls of DTP typography—not only for PostScript on the Mac platform, but for PostScript and PCL on the PC platform too. Whatever your current configuration, *Desktop Typographics* will address your needs. Also included are comprehensive resources on professional associations, periodicals, and books that can help you further your professional development in this rapidly evolving field.

I have tried to make this book as easy to understand as possible, given the complex nature of its subject, and to keep it always sensitive to the real business-oriented demands of the working world. To the many companies who supplied information, and the many colleagues who added the wisdom of their expertise, I give my thanks.

To you, the reader, I offer my sincere best wishes for success in your publishing endeavors and for a growing appreciation of the preciousness of the written word.

Acknowledgments

Excerpts from *Information Anxiety* by Richard Saul Wurman, copyright ©1989 by Richard Saul Wurman. Used by permission of Doubleday, a division of Bantam Doubleday Dell Publishing Group, Inc.

Excerpts from *Desktop Publishing: The Awful Truth* by Jeffrey Parnau, copyright ©1989 by Jeffrey Parnau. Used by permission of Parnau Graphics Incorporated.

The list of Typographic Industry Terms and Conditions of Sale is used by permission of the Typographers International Association (TIA).

Illustration credits

Chapter 1
Pages 15, 16, 18, 23: AGFA Compugraphic
Pages 17, 19: Bitstream Inc.
Page 21: Allotype Typographics, Ann Arbor, MI

Chapter 2
Pages 36, 37, 38: ALSoft, Inc.
Page 39 top: Elfring Soft Fonts
Page 39 bottom: Roxxolid

Page 40: ETI Software Corp.; Ross Virostko—President, Rick Rocheleau—Programmer, Diane Avellano—Manager of Sales, Mark Goren—CEO

Pages 41, 42: Jeffrey Shulman

Chapter 3

Pages 45, 46, 48, 49, 50: Altsys Corporation

Page 51 top: Screen capture of bitmap and outline editors in Publisher's Type Foundry®. Used by permission of Z-Soft Corporation. Publisher's Type Foundry is a registered trademark of Z-Soft Corporation.

Page 51 bottom: Design Science

Chapter 4

Page 54 top three: Broderbund

Page 54 bottom two, 55 bottom: SoftCraft

Page 55 top two: Images created using Arts & Letters by Computer Support Corp., Dallas, TX

Chapter 5

Page 60: Pairs Software

Page 61: Copyright 1989, 1990 ICOM Simulations, Inc. MacKern is a trademark of ICOM Simulations, Inc. MacKern screenshot is used with permission.

Chapter 6

Page 68: Promontory Systems

Chapter 7

Page 73: Ultimate Technographics

Page 75: ElseWare

Chapter 8

Page 85: Shana Corporation

Page 86, 87, 89: Digital Composition Systems

Before You Begin

Welcome to *Desktop Typographics*!

I have been a typographer for ten years and before that, a graphic designer for five years. Most recently, I have been writing about type, desktop publishing, and the graphic arts. Everything I know about these three fields, I taught myself: by reading, by talking to people, by attending presentations, and, especially, by doing.

There is no secret to success beyond a willingness to learn and to do hard work. The same opportunities are there for you too.

Many people in our society know how to be taught, but few have discovered how to learn on their own. *Desktop Typographics* will help you in your quest to understand desktop publishing and to use it in achieving your communication goals.

This book will not try to tell you all there is to know about desktop typography. Considering how quickly the field is developing, no one can claim to be the ultimate authority.

Naturally, you must participate actively in reading this book, in the sense that you should question, reject, or adapt the information you find here, based on your own interest, creativity, and experience. By the same token, *Desktop Typographics* is not the only book you need to understand this complex topic. Just the opposite is true.

Rather than trying to present all the answers, *Desktop Typographics* tries to help you ask the right questions.

This book presents insights and interpretations on type in DTP, with the aim of clarifying how things work, how to pick the right processes and products for your needs, how to make use of the skills of others in the field (such as service bureaus), and how to make all these things fit together. It also presents as many resources as possible on the subject of type in the desktop-publishing environment.

It is up to you to follow your own interest, test what is presented here against your own situation, and discover your own path to the mastery of desktop publishing.

I realized I didn't have to know everything, just know where and how to find it.
Richard Saul Wurman,
INFORMATION ANXIETY

About this book

Desktop publishing is a complex field that has revolutionized the way we look at the whole process of getting words and images into print.

Desktop Typographics is a complete overview of everything you need to know to work with type in today's electronic-publishing environment—the art of typography, font technology, enhancements, and the business of typesetting. Also included are many extremely important resource lists you can use to get additional information about various topics.

The aim of this book is to be concise, complete, and easy to use. The information is presented in a step-by-step format, for hands-on use in the real world. Wherever relevant, the text is illustrated with typographic examples, diagrams, photographs, and flowcharts.

On the other hand, there is a lot of information you will not find here, and that is one of the book's strengths. *Desktop Typographics* does not cover the topics of writing, graphic design, typographic history, outdated typesetting technologies, photography, illustration, or offset printing.

Similarly, it is not intended as a program manual, a critique of specific hardware or software packages, a guide to using images in your DTP documents, or a guide to presentation graphics. However, this does not mean that the skills and resources you will gain from reading this book will not be applicable to your own business relationships. An understanding of and appreciation for the graphic arts' heritage is an essential ingredient in successful business communication, in addition to being something that enriches our enjoyment of those pursuits; it is just not the focus of this book.

Where do you fit in?

If you are reading this book, you probably already have some experience with desktop publishing. You may be a single-station user, producing your own publications from start to finish, or you may be part of a large communications department, working with others in a network to produce a wide range of documents in many forms. Either way, you have probably found the field exciting in its possibilities and frustrating in its complexity.

Three principles are close to my heart: accepting ignorance, paying attention to questions, and going in the opposite direction.
R. Wurman

How you use DTP depends on who you are. Each type of publishing activity has its own demands and restrictions. The first step in successful implementation of an electronic-publishing system is figuring out where you fit in.

Noncommercial applications

Noncommercial applications can include any publishing integral to an organization's internal administration. The publications can range from corporate literature, financial reports, technical documentation, manuals, bulletins, newsletters, and forms to items even intended for sale or distribution to customers. The key issue in these applications is improving the existing production cycles of document management.

Input in this situation comes as text from authors and as data from various microcomputer sources and/or a host-computer database. Composition includes text entry and formatting, data-driven business graphics, and technical information, all made up into pages. Output is generally to both electronic archive and laser printer for eventual duplication. In the case of database publishing, form and content can be dealt with in very different fashions.

Commercial applications

In commercial applications, the final product is intended specifically for sale to customers. Books, magazines, and newspapers are the usual examples. However, commercial applications also include any field that ties in with commercial industries (such as advertising, packaging, and graphic design) and/or any project in which high visual appeal is an issue.

The key issues in commercial applications are rigorous standards of quality, control, and flexibility.

Input often includes not only text from various sources, but also art, all of which may come in many different formats, and all of which may require different kinds of processing by different people. Composition involves design-intensive layouts that change frequently, tight deadlines, and use of outside services. Output involves sophisticated imagesetters and perhaps color separators for eventual printing, binding, and large-scale distribution.

Different needs, different solutions

"Publishing" is not the only area where DTP is used. When you think about it, you'll find publishing skills are a part of many projects. Whenever we communicate on paper, slides, or overhead transparencies, one on one or in the classroom, we see ourselves as publishers.

As you can see from even this very basic breakdown, everyone needs something unique from desktop-publishing technologies.

There is one theme, however, that runs through the whole spectrum of DTP applications: careful planning and constant assessment of results. Trying to evaluate desktop-publishing systems and products can be full of traps.

One difficulty is that DTP vendors would like you to believe not only that DTP is always superior to conventional production techniques, but also that one system can "do it all" for you. Another problem is that the information you really need is often difficult to find. Even when you find it, it's often hard to understand.

And as if those two problems were not big enough barriers in themselves, there is also the problem of having to rise above the details of DTP to see the big picture.

The first step in overcoming these hurdles is to accept that you do not have to know and do everything yourself. Be selective.

The next step is to evaluate your DTP needs from a larger perspective.

DTP and the publishing process

The fact of the matter is that learning to use DTP technologies is no substitute for understanding and mastering the many skills required to publish effectively— writing, editing, graphic design, typography, illustration, composition, layout, pre-press, printing, and distribution, not to mention the management of resources, personnel, and money. It is only one more skill in a very complex process involving many people.

The key issue here is seeing desktop publishing from the perspective of the graphic arts as a whole. Learning a

DTP system will not guarantee success in itself. You must also learn about publication design and production.

Publication design

What is publication design? It is the logical arrangement of information into levels of meaning. It is the skeleton that gives form to facts and makes their relationship clear to the reader. This logical arrangement can be called an information hierarchy.

Many publications have pictures and graphics in them, but rarely do they convey their primary message through images. Type is the one element common to all printed and televised news communications, and perhaps it is the most important.

You may look at a publication that has good type and poor images, and you will be forgiving. But no matter how fantastic the images are, if the typography is poor and the information hierarchy is unclear, you will not give the piece more than a couple of seconds of your time.

That's why learning to use type effectively is probably the single most powerful skill you can acquire in desktop publishing. And that's why *Desktop Typographics* was written.

For many people in the desktop-publishing environment, publication design is the weakest link in their skill repertoire. This is perfectly understandable, since many DTP users come from an office background, rather than from the graphic arts. People with a nonpublishing background tend to have very high expectations of DTP, and though DTP gives them the promise of being able to create powerful designs for their documents and an overabundance of technical tools, DTP manuals offer very little in the way of publication design expertise.

To play the piano, you must practice the piano. The same holds true for writing, artwork, layout, design, and all the other disciplines associated with professional publishing. Computer experience is an additional skill— not the only skill.
Jeffrey Parnau,
DTP: THE AWFUL TRUTH

Publication production

Publication design is only half the battle. The other half is integrating DTP into the wider world of pre-press and printing. That's why a large part of *Desktop Typographics* is devoted to print production with DTP tools.

For those from a graphic arts background, the task is a little easier. With their previous exposure to conventional methods, they at least have some yardstick by which to measure the strengths and weaknesses of DTP technology. But for beginners, it is another story.

Every DTP user, however, is in the same boat when it comes to making DTP systems work. First of all, no DTP product is free of bugs: technical problems are bound to happen in any installation. Nothing is perfect. Secondly, and just as important, no DTP product can manage every step of the publishing process. When you start to mix and match programs or use outside services, you are going to have compatibility problems for sure.

In fact, one whole segment of the electronic publishing business is devoted entirely to solving just these kinds of problems. There are numerous programs out there designed specifically to help other programs live up to their sales claims! There are also lots of machines and programs designed specifically to help other machines and programs understand one another.

Desktop Typographics will give you the map you need to navigate this complex territory: building a system, font technologies, integrating text and graphics, interface to typesetting, working with color, output options, and dealing with service bureaus are all covered.

Create a master plan before attempting to install a DTP system. Use a ladder approach and attempt to achieve a single goal at a time. Forget the sales claims.
J. Parnau

The business of desktop publishing

People, time, and money are as much a part of successful DTP as hardware and software. Training, scheduling,

budgeting, and working with others are all covered in
relation to the various topics.

All in all, *Desktop Typographics* is written to be as
responsive as possible to the demands of using DTP in the
business world. Whatever your place in desktop
publishing and whatever your typographic requirements,
this book will serve you well.

A word about the platforms

The world of DTP falls into two major categories based
on platforms: Macintosh or PC. Each environment has its
own special advantages and disadvantages.

At first glance, it would seem that the larger portion of
users today employ Mac systems. But on closer
investigation, that turns out only to be the case in the
commercial-publishing field. In corporate publishing, IBM
and Hewlett-Packard have colossal customer bases. For
those users, PCs are the way to go.

The PC market is further divided into use of Adobe's
PostScript or Hewlett-Packard's PCL as a document
description language. Bitmap fonts and enhancement
programs, for all their limitations, also play a significant
role in both Macintosh and PC markets.

Desktop Typographics groups its contents along these
lines. Unless otherwise noted, the information pertains to
Macintosh. PC features, products, and so on are divided
into PostScript and PCL categories. In cases where a
particular company markets essentially the same product
to both markets, some mention of this will be made.

Some products require a more powerful platform than
just the basic Mac or PC. Lots of hard disk space,
extended or expanded random-access memory (RAM),
and math coprocessors are the typical upgrades required.
Space limitations do not permit the inclusion of specific
model requirements for the products listed, but that

GROUND RULES FOR EFFECTIVE PRINTED COMMUNICATION

The lessons of history

Publishing has been around a
long time, and there is a wealth
of information on how to do it
effectively. In the course of its
evolution, we have developed a
wide range of traditions and
conventions to help us produce
and understand printed
publications easily. You may
choose to ignore these lessons
of history, but you do so at
your own risk.

Rule number one

Careful planning and constant
assessment of results are major
factors in your communications
strategy. Set clearly defined,
attainable goals for yourself.
Look at all your options before
you commit to something, and
do not be afraid to change if
things are not working.

Rule number two

Developing good writing and editing skills is essential in getting your point across. No matter what you are trying to say, no one is going to take you very seriously if you cannot spell, cannot write a proper sentence, or cannot follow a logical train of thought.

Rule number three

The key to effective publication design is a clear, instructive, and appropriate structure for your information. The medium may not be the message, but it has a profound impact on how the message will be received.

Rule number four

Always take into consideration how a piece will be printed while you are developing your copy and design. Print production is the last step of the publishing cycle before distribution, but the particular printing method you use will impose important limitations right back through the whole creative process of design.

information can generally be found in the products' sales literature.

A word about the product lists

Manufacturers' suggested retail list prices are used throughout this text. They are given in U.S. dollars, for the U.S. market, unless otherwise noted (particularly for products originating in Canada).

Mastering electronic publishing is inextricably linked to specific products. While, in the Macintosh environment, most programs tend to look and act the same way, that is not the case with PC environments. There, products can be very different.

For both followings, the "productization" of the market can sometimes be a disadvantage, in that vendors may tend to generate demand for the specific features being offered rather than to address real needs.

To link specific products and features would perhaps have made a more timely book than does the format followed in this book, but it would then suffer from abbreviated usefulness as products are updated or supplanted by others. The major advantage of the book's generic approach is that, without playing favorites, it provides a comprehensive overview of all the major issues you will need to understand as you progress in your desktop journey. Each chapter also contains one or more product lists of relevent hardware and software. The Vendors appendix at the back of the book will tell you where to order sales literature on items that interest you.

A word about truth in advertising

The research material for this book was gathered by soliciting sales literature or samples for every product mentioned. The brochures fill a large filing box. The books, periodicals, and programs run to almost ten feet of shelf space.

Reading between the lines in sales literature is an art. For any product that interests you, get the competitors' brochures as well. You will be surprised at the differences that can come to light on close inspection of the material.

For example, one brochure may devote lots of space to technical specifications, compatibility, and so on. Another may say nothing at all on those topics. Some companies with glossy advertising have inferior products; other companies with very ugly advertising have excellent, indispensible products.

By the same token, graphic user interfaces, manuals, and user support can also vary widely.

For the most part, products in any one category tend to be about the same price, but sometimes one or two products will be radically above or below the price point. It is important to know why.

In short, read the literature, make up a list of questions and phone the vendor with them, and set up a demo. For the demo, it is important to bring along some of your actual text and graphic files. Compatibility is crucial. No product is worth anything if it cannot handle your data format.

Resource networks for product recommendations and purchasing decisions are an equally important part of your information gathering.

What we choose to read and what we choose to ignore are...some of the most critical decisions we make, yet they are invariably made with little thought, almost unconsciously.
R. Wurman

The only sure way to know if what you want to do is actually possible is to see it in action. Don't buy on promises. If the sales force can't show it to you, [to be safe] assume that it can't be done.
J. Parnau

A word about liability and trademarks

The information in this book is distributed on an "as is" basis, without warranty. While every effort has been made in the preparation of this book to ensure the accuracy of the information, neither the author nor the publisher shall have any responsibility to any person or entity with respect to any liability, loss, or damage caused or alleged to be caused directly or indirectly by the instructions contained in this book or by the computer software and hardware products described herein. It remains the responsibility of users to apply their professional knowledge in the use of information contained in this book, to consult original sources for additional information when necessary, and to employ professional guidance when appropriate.

Throughout the book, trademarked names are used. Rather than put a trademark symbol in every occurrence of a trademarked name, we state that we are using the names only in an editorial fashion and to the benefit of the trademark owner with no intention of infringement of the trademark.

CHAPTER ONE

Fonts: Your Basic Building Blocks

What is a font, anyway? Different people define *font* in various ways: one typeface family, one size and style, one orientation, one file format, resolution. These are all possible definitions.

This book defines a font as one typeface in one style, with the necessary digital backup to make it work.

Because scaling fonts on the fly is now the norm in electronic publishing, size is really no longer such a big issue in distinguishing different fonts. Mind you, for those installations still using bitmap fonts, screens or printers unable to scale fonts, or other constraints, font definition must also include discrete point size and orientation (portrait/landscape) too.

The plethora of output devices and interpretive drivers makes specifying a font by its media tricky as well. Fonts come on floppies, hard disks, and CD-ROM, over the phone, and from scanners.

A font generally contains three types of files: printer, screen instructions, and font metrics files. In certain media formats, font metrics may be contained as part of the basic font file. Many also include a download utility as part of the package.

The next section examines some of the ins and outs of fonts.

Characters in search of a play

We normally think of our alphabet as having 26 letters. In fact, our palette is much more varied than that; it offers the possibility of great subtlety and nuance. There are capital and lowercase letters, punctuation, figures (including superiors, inferiors, and fractions), and commonly used symbols and ornaments. A complete font can contain up to 250-odd elements.

The selection of type styles—roman, italic, bold, small caps, swash, and so on—increases your options. There is no one standard for how many styles you will find in a given font family. It can range from one to more than thirty, but four (roman, italic, bold, bold italic) is the typical minimum for all except specialty faces.

You can also buy specialized fonts for science, mathematics, or foreign language work (including non-Latin alphabets). These fonts offer characters and features you cannot find anywhere else.

The International Standards Organization (ISO) has been working to develop a font description that is vendor- and system-independent. But because they are trying to create a standard that will apply to font resources and font references at the same time, it is a complicated process.

One thing the ISO has agreed on, however, is certain commonly used character sets for fonts. In North America, the ISO Latin 1 character set is normative. It

FONT: One typeface of a family, in one particular weight, style, and character set. Size is no longer a font limitation in electronic publishing, and it is thus no longer a component of fonts. It has been replaced by font metrics.

FONT METRICS: The mathematical structure of characters and their relationships.

BITMAP FONTS: Built dot by dot. They come in one point size and lose definition when enlarged, reduced, or modified. They are hard to edit.

SCALABLE FONTS: Built with outline vector graphics. They keep fidelity at all sizes and orientations.

PRINTER FONT: The outline format used to make the actual output.

SCREEN FONT: The version you see on your computer screen. It is composed of pixels.

DOWNLOAD: Managerial function describing the transmission of an operating routine or of data to a peripheral device or party.

UPLOAD: Input of data (such as fonts, text, or graphics) or programs from an outside source.

contains 227 characters, including free-floating diacriticals, numerous accented characters, common symbols, and so on.

Other character sets

ISO Latin 1 is not the only popular character set. Others include ASCII (127 characters), USASCII (96 characters), EuroASCII, Roman 8 (192 characters), Ventura 8, several legal sets, special matrix, scientific, PC graphics, line draw, tax line draw, numerous kinds of bar codes, OCR-A, and OCR-B.

While some of these configurations are commonly found in every kind of typesetting situation, others are required for unique situations. For example, typefaces with proportional spacing are most likely to feature the first seven character sets mentioned above. Specialized character sets usually involve fixed spacing.

Vendors often give you more elements in a font than you will normally need. It is relatively easy to create condensed character sets for speed and efficiency with some of the font management tools described in the following chapters.

Sometimes, however, memory restrictions (especially in combination font cartridges) force font vendors to reduce the number of characters in a typeface in order to fit more typefaces or variations into the package. It is possible to create missing characters and insert them into the font yourself after the fact, but that is a laborious process.

If hard disk space is an important issue for you, remember that there are several font management programs currently available that will condense the memory requirements of your screen fonts. With other programs, you can keep your fonts right off your hard drive altogether and still carry on with a minimum of fuss.

New developments in screen font technology (such as Type Manager from Adobe and TrueType from

A character may appear in many different forms before it reaches its final destination. Let's look at some of them. First, a clean outline of the character made from Bezier curves. This is the standard of precision you should be striving for in offset-printed documents.

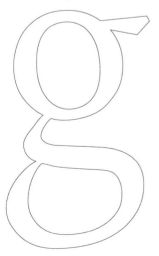

Apple/MicroSoft) mean that you do not need to create many discrete point sizes for screen fonts any more.

The bottom line on all this is that when you have a choice, go for more characters in a font, even if you do not plan to use them very much.

An enlarged view of a bitmap version of the same character, in the same face (AGFA Compugraphic's Garth Graphic), taken from a 24-point original. This level of legibility is suitable for laser-printed documents.

The quest for elegant typography

Until recently, typefaces could not be copyrighted. There are certain recognized font foundries who license their faces to multiple font vendors, but it is possible to use clone faces too. Many typefaces exist in multiple versions from different manufacturers. The letterforms are slightly modified; the fit is different and so are the character sets. Older faces, like Garamond or Century, may go under the same name. More recent faces assume aliases to protect the not-so-innocent. Helvetica, for example, is available in at least six popular analogs.

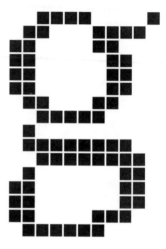

Font metrics

Some analog type designs suffer horribly at the hands of inept tinkerers, even if the characters are well cut. A "good" face is often ruined by a poorly thought out font format file, even though the results may be hard to detect without an actual sample.

Tracking and kerning remain two hallmarks of fine typography. But fonts vary widely in their handling of these crucial ingredients.

Good fonts come with sensible kerning data resources, a subject all in itself. (See Chapter Five, Kerning.)

Resolution hints improve the legibility of laser-printed characters in small point sizes. Using an enlarged view of a character from Bitstream's 18-point Snell Roundhand as an example, here is a comparison between unhinted and hinted versions. The small dots represent dots per inch: the points at which the laser in your laser printer's imaging engine may or may not fire. The large black squares represent the points at which it would actually fire, according to the font metrics and hinting information it is given.

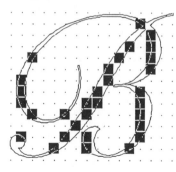

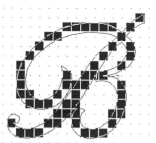

Hints and secrets

There are often several versions of a single typeface from any one vendor. For example, the vendor may offer a unique feature in a font and protect that feature with proprietary encryption.

For example, Adobe offers Type 1 and Type 3 fonts to the public. Type 1 fonts were encrypted until recently and could only be used with specific licensing, equipment, and software packages. Type 3 fonts were more flexible, but lacked the resolution hints that made Type 1 fonts worth protecting.

Resolution hints are printer commands that optimize the appearance of type depending on the output medium. For example, type off a laser printer in small point sizes requires intervention in stroke positioning for legibility.

Monotype also offers resolution hints on their fonts, which it licenses to other font foundries as Nimbus Q. Fonts from Kingsley/ATF include an optional optical scaling feature that compensates for weight and position when drawing strokes in different sizes.

With the advent of Apple's System 7 and TrueType font format (formerly known as Royal Font), Adobe has chosen to publish its Type 1 format, making it available to original equipment manufacturers (OEMs). The end result for users is twofold: first, Type 1 fonts are now available from a broader selection of font vendors; second, many programs that previously could not handle Adobe Type 1 fonts now can. You will have to look for those specific upgrades when shopping for fonts and font enhancements.

These are certainly not the only file formats on the market. In fact, there are more vendors in the font category than any other. Bitstream and Compugraphic, to name two large presences, have been successfully offering alternatives in PostScript and PCL typography for some time. Among the many, many other smaller font foundries, proprietary file formats abound.

Applications supported

When you are buying a font, it is very important to know if it will work with your system. Do not assume that it will.

Platform, medium, program, memory size, printer configuration, screen resolution, and many other factors must be considered. This is especially true in the PCL environment. For example, you may want to look for PCL fonts that come with drivers for Windows, PageMaker, and/or Ventura Publisher.

Company support

In researching this book, more than 250 companies were consulted. Some were extremely helpful and efficient. Others were labyrinths of reclusive employees who seemed never to talk to each other. Unfortunately, this corporate side of things did not directly relate to the quality of the products. That would have made the job easier. As it was, even the simplest request to send information sometimes took a formal letter and four phone calls to different people before the material finally arrived. Getting knowledgable phone help about technical issues was only marginally easier.

You do not want to find yourself in a similar situation, having already bought somebody's font.

Sales literature can sometimes be an indication of market responsiveness, but in a perverse kind of way. It is sometimes the larger companies with successful products who have difficulty responding to individuals with specialized needs. On the other end of the spectrum, small companies may leave you high and dry when it comes to answers.

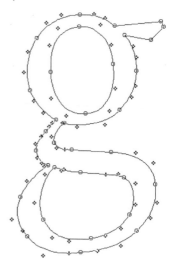

Another type of outline version editable by a drawing program (FreeHand), showing Bezier points.

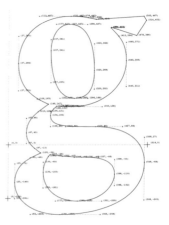

Using a font-editing program (Fontographer), you can see not only the Bezier control points, but also their numerical values.

DISPLAY FACES: Feature highly stylized characters. They are most commonly used for headlines.

Libraries

Typefaces get grouped into style ghettoes from time to time. There are book faces, report faces, display faces, and eccentrics.

Font vendors vary in their respective audiences, and so their type catalogues show marked biases. It is generally advisable to think of buying families of typefaces rather than individual styles. Display faces are the exception.

It is a cruel twist of fate that many font vendors specialize in display faces that are ugly, unreadable, and extremely limited in their usefulness.

Stick to buying typefaces that you will use a lot. Unless you have a specific need only one vendor can fill, build your library from companies that have a strong ongoing commitment to the highest standards of typography. Many of these companies offer enhanced versions of fonts for high-end clients.

Fonts and service bureaus

Bitstream uses a slightly different way of editing new type designs. This intermediate form shows perpendiculars to tangents at all Bezier control points.

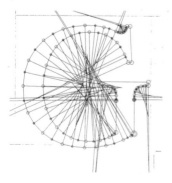

If you are planning to use a service bureau for final output, perhaps on an imagesetter, find out what fonts the service bureau offers. If it does not have exactly the same fonts you are using, in the same versions from the same vendor, you will have to send your fonts along with your job. Bear in mind that running off your job without any modification is a limited service. The results are only as good as you make them. For a typographer to go into your file and perform some typographic fine-tuning, you need to give them at least the fonts, if not the host program. This can get complicated. Most of the service bureaus consulted in researching this book said that, for the most part, they either create the jobs themselves from scratch, with their own fonts, or they simply run out what has been given them.

The service bureaus were also asked what percentage of clients send files and fonts, requesting the service bureau to go in and clean things up or perform further processing. The answer was "5 to 10 percent but growing."

Where page makeup programs are part of a larger electronic pre-press situation, perhaps outputting to a color separation system, font compatibility becomes much more critical.

Conversely, presentation graphics and animated TV typography have their own requirements and standards, which are not addressed in this book.

The market orientation of service bureaus itself has significant bearing on the percentages mentioned above, but that is dealt with more completely in Chapter Twelve, Service Bureaus.

Fonts and other programs

Font compatibility goes beyond hardware and environment. Your ability to benefit from font managers, font editors, special effects, kerning programs, formware, and database publishing all depend on what kind of font format you are using.

For example, many drawing programs, font editors, and special effects programs allow you to alter the shape of a character by reading its outline, translating it into an editable format, and then exporting it to another document. Some fonts come with this format already included in the font metrics files. In some cases, this process turns the text block(s) into a graphic that cannot be edited with a word processor; in other cases, it does not.

Many enhancement programs only work with fonts from a specific vendor (often the one selling the enhancement).

PROPORTIONAL SPACING: In fonts with proportional spacing, each character has a unique width.

FIXED SPACING: In fonts with fixed spacing, every character has the same width.

ANALOG FONTS: Almost identical versions of design and font metrics from different manufacturers.

FONT FORMAT FILE: Another common term for font metrics.

TRACKING: The consistent removal of white space between characters in a line of type.

KERNING: The selective removal of white space between discrete character pairs in a line of type.

ZERO-ESCAPEMENT CHARACTERS: Usually the carriage advances after a character is printed. Zero-escapement characters, however, are "flash-only" and have no width for position calculations.

TRANSLITERATION: Substitution of non-Latin characters on the screen and output for Latin characters on the keyboard.

LOCALIZED SCRIPT MANAGERS: With these, all on-screen program information appears in a language other than English.

Fonts may contain many things besides your basic alphabet. These examples of scientific fonts from Allotype include symbols for applications in mathematics and chemistry.

Thompson

abcdefghijklmnopqrstuvwxyz
1234567890ç-=[]\',./≡!@#$%•&*()_+{}|:"<>?
ABCDEFGHIJKLMNOPQRSTUVWXYZ
αβξδ⟨φγη•∂κλμ≡øπθρστςωχψζ
˜ ˆ áÍ∞§†˙ ¨ ˚ ≠→|≈⌡˙ ⌒↔
ÁÏΞΔεΦΓ⁊ιⱱÒΛÓⱱØΠΘΝΣΥυÌΩÙΨÚÇ
˜ˆ ÂÎ∝È‡¨˙ ¨˙ —±→|-ƒ˜‴⇌

Structure

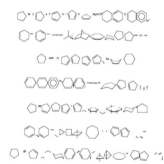

Getting your document from the screen to the printer in finished form is the acid test. That process can have many stages. But choosing fonts is the first critical step.

Specialty fonts

Do you speak multilingual or scientese? If so, this subject is for you. There is much more to foreign language typesetting than meets the eye. The same holds true in typesetting for chemistry, physics, mathematics, music, and other specialized fields.

It is not enough to have the necessary characters and accents to do the job. Sometimes a right-to-left reading is needed. Zero-escapement characters and formulas can necessitate complex spacing outside the scope of many desktop publishing programs. Keyboard remapping, software-selectable keyboards, super-efficient keyboard interpreters, automatic alphabetical sorting order, and other enhancements such as macros, automated transliteration, or localized script managers may also be required.

Specialty fonts often have different prices depending on what platform, program, and printer are being driven, and their compatibility is relatively limited. But in some cases, they offer the most powerful tools for the specific work they do.

The impact of resolution on font designs

Impact serial printers print about 80 dots per inch (dpi). Laser printers print between 300 and 1000 dpi. Their typical dpi range is 300 to 400.

Imagesetters use lasers to expose photographic paper or film directly. Unlike laser printers, they do not require application of toner powder and heat processing.

The result of using photo rather than toner technology is a much more exact image, a much higher resolution, and a different method of calculating that resolution. When talking about imagesetters, we talk about resolution in lines per inch (referring to the number of raster scans the laser beam makes per inch). Many graphic arts professionals consider 1000 lines per inch to be the minimum worthy of being called high-resolution, although some imagesetters can set even higher resolutions.

This should not be confused with lines-per-minute speed rating. In that case, the line referred to is a line of type 9/10 by 11 picas, or thereabouts. The number of these lines a machine can output in one minute is its rated speed.

When it comes to imaging modern documents, speed is measured entirely differently. A complex file with images may take many minutes, or even hours, to run off. Again, that's an issue best left for another chapter.

In any event, when a designer is creating a new typeface, it is necessary to take into consideration the probable end form it will take. Legibility and readability are affected by resolution, and it is often a trade-off as to which will get preference: quality or speed.

For example, let's say your laser printer operates at 300 dpi. But the toner powder is not nearly so precise. That's why some fonts come with resolution hints: to improve legibility of laser printer output in small point sizes. But typefaces can be designed to look their best in one medium or another (screen, laser printer, imagesetter). Something that looks badly spaced off a laser printer can be just fine when viewed at a much higher resolution. The reverse is also true.

Here is another example. Dropping type out of a black background or image is increasingly common in desktop typography. The results can sometimes be a surprise.

A laser beam flashes on a point as a circle. Half the beam is past the cutoff point, and this is accounted for in

DOT: One dot on your laser printer output. There can be anywhere from 300 to 1000 dots to the horizontal inch.

LINE: One line on your imagesetter. There can be anywhere from 1000 to 4000 lines to the horizontal inch.

PIXEL: One dot on your computer screen. There are usually 72 pixels to the horizontal inch.

VIDEOTEX: Documents specifically designed to be used on computer screens only.

the design of the font. But when you shoot a negative image, the result can look lighter or heavier than the original, depending on how your program deals with the "extra" piece of the laser beam on the end point of the scan line. Some imagesetters can compensate for this, but others cannot. Laser printers do not.

Some faces, like Lucida, were designed specifically for laser printers. Each output environment has its own possibilities and restrictions. The day is coming when type will likely end up being read as much on-line from a computer screen as it is from paper—for example, in videotex applications. Designing fonts for this medium requires an entirely different set of standards.

Looking to the future

All in all, most current developments in electronic publishing are focusing on the graphics side of the equation (as opposed to type) and on joining together applications that previously stood alone.

Granted, font technology will continue to go through upgrades, modifications, and enhancements. But for the most part, that change is not going to mean your current font library is soon to be out of date.

This chapter is somewhat unique, in that fonts have been a part of typesetting for hundreds of years. The conventions of typography are well defined and the general publishing public is rapidly becoming more sensitive to them. We have some points of reference.

In later chapters, this book will cover programs and capabilities exclusive to the world of desktop publishing. Fasten your seat belt, you are about to leave the known universe.

It is not recommend that you read this book cover to cover, unless you have an iron constitution and a photographic memory. Better yet, make that a database

However a character is created, and whatever it looks like in editable form, ultimately you want it to look as sharp and beautiful as this.

memory, because desktop typography will sometimes leave you feeling more confused than Alice in Wonderland. *Desktop Typographics* will give you the map you need to arrive at your communication destination.

POSTSCRIPT: A page description language developed by Adobe Systems. PostScript fonts are scalable, may contain resolution hints, and are built with vector graphics. PostScript is equally versatile with text and graphics.

Mac and PC—PostScript

Adobe Fonts *(Adobe Systems)*
106 volumes / $185 per volume (4 fonts) / $95–$370, price range

AgfaType *(AGFA Compugraphic)*
Professional Series: PostScript fonts / 127 volumes, 532 fonts / $169 per volume (3 or 4 fonts) / $90–$340, price range / Studio Series: Editable PostScript outline fonts / 75 volumes, 298 fonts / $169 per volume

Fluent Laser Fonts *(Casady & Greene)*
22 volumes / $89.95 per volume (3-5 fonts)

Fontware *(Bitstream)*
1000 fonts / $45 per font (minimum order 4 fonts) / $195 each: Symbols 1, Headlines combo packs / $395 each: Fundamentals Series, including collections for newsletters, books and manuals, and flyers

KeyCap Fonts *(Paperback Software)*
$149.95 complete

Linotype Library *(Linotype)*
157 volumes, 600 fonts / $185 per volume (4 fonts) / $95–$370, price range

Monotype Classic Type *(Monotype USA)*
65 volumes, 275 fonts / $150 per volume (4 fonts)

Music Font Series *(Coda Music Software)*
4 volumes: transcription fonts / $69 each / 1 volume:
DTP music publishing fonts / $149

Publishing Pack 1: Newsletters *(Adobe Systems)*
$395

Publishing Pack 2: Forms and Schedules *(Adobe Systems)*
$475

Publishing Pack 3: Presentations *(Adobe Systems)*
$475

Mac—PostScript

A*1 Prospera with Italic, A*1 Egyptian Bold Condensed
(Alphabets)
$74.95 Prospera / $59.95 Egyptian

Adobe Collector's Edition: Patterns & Textures *(Adobe Systems)*
$225

Adobe Collector's Edition: Symbols, Borders, & Letterforms *(Adobe Systems)*
$125

Allotype Fonts *(Allotype Typographics)*
3 science fonts, 1 design font (4 styles), 2 Greek fonts, 2
Polish fonts (4 styles each) / $75 Haber/Thompson
science fonts / $125 Structures chemical structure font /
$160 Haber/Thompson/Structures / $40 Tempora (small
caps version of LaserWriter Times) / $85 Kadmos,
Demotiki, Czasy, or Szwajcarskie

ATF Classic Type *(Kingsley/ATF)*
Digitizing 180-year-old library of more than 20,000
protected designs, including typefaces, borders, and
ornaments / $195 per volume (4 fonts)

Bill's Picture Fonts *(U-Design Type Foundry)*
4 fonts

Bullets & Boxes *(Casey's Page Mill)*
1 symbol font / $89

ClickArt LaserLetters *(T/Maker)*
3 volumes / $79.95 each

Faces *(Altsys)*
16 volumes of fonts, 4 volumes of borders, 1 volume of
ornaments / $79.95 per volume, fonts / $59.95 each,
borders or ornaments

Fonts *(Ecological Linguistics)*
68 foreign fonts (Latin- and non-Latin-based) / $90–$120
per font / $60–$80 per font for home use / 50%
surcharge per font for multiple users / extra charges for
modified system files, application files, and/or
alphabetical sorting

Font Sets I & II *(EmDash)*
2 volumes, 18 fonts / $63 per volume

Lanston Type Library *(Giampa Textware)*
Digitizing library of 16,000 fonts / 7 volumes currently available / $165 Albertan No. 977 (4 styles) / $70 Goudy Thirty, No. 392 (with swash) / $65 Hadriano Title No. 309 / $65 Jenson No. 58 / $165 Kaatskill (Goudy) No. 976 (4 styles) / $75 Leaf ornaments (128 characters) / $65 Swing Bold No. 217 / $450 Goudy Illuminated Initials (26 characters)

LaserFONTS *(Linguist's Software)*
37 volumes: foreign, non-Latin, math fonts / $49.95–$149.95 per volume

LASERgenix *(Devonian International)*
6 volumes: Cyrillic, phonetic, fraction fonts / $39.50 per volume

LetraFont *(Letraset)*
139 fonts / $75 per font

MacFontware *(Bitstream)*
10 volumes / $169 per volume (4 fonts)

PIXymbols *(Page Studio Graphics)*
20 volumes: various keyboard and graphic symbol sets / $40–$95 per volume

PostScript Type for the Macintosh *(Mactography)*
16 volumes / $79–$129 per volume

Professional PostScript Fonts *(Digital Typeface Corporation)*
750 volumes, 1350 fonts / $169.95 per volume

Studio231 Fonts *(Studio 231)*
20 volumes / $99 per volume (6 fonts)

Typeface Library *(Image Club Graphics)*
600 licensed fonts / $25 per font

World Class Laser Type *(Dubl-Click)*
7 volumes: text fonts (3 fonts in each), 2 volumes:
graphics fonts (2 fonts in each) / $79.95 per volume

Mac—Bitmap

ARTFONTS *(Tactic Software)*
3 volumes / $49.50 per volume (6 fonts)

Bill's Dingbats *(U-Design Type Foundry)*
Shareware $8 / Box Specials $49.95 / Universal Symbols
$49.95 / Barnhart Ornaments $39.95

Bitstream SoftFonts for the Macintosh *(Bitstream)*
35 LaserWriter–equivalent fonts / $195 13-font set /
$295 22-font extension set / $395 35-font set

cgType Typefaces for the Macintosh *(AGFA
Compugraphic)*
80 volumes / $169 per volume (4 fonts)

ClickArt Letters 1 & 2 *(T/Maker)*
2 volumes (17 and 16 fonts, respectively) / $49.95 per
volume

18 + Fonts *(18 + Fonts)*
5 fonts

Faces *(Altsys)*
8 volumes / $39.95 per volume

Fluent Fonts *(Casady & Greene)*
66 fonts (1–3 point sizes per font) / $49.95 complete

FONTagenix *(Devonian International)*
4 volumes text and graphic fonts / $39.95 per volume
(average 12 fonts)

Fonts *(Budgetbytes)*
34 disks bitmap fonts (each with up to 28 fonts in 1 or 2
sizes) / 12 disks laser fonts / public domain and
shareware products / $3.19 400K disk / $5.99 800K disk

Fonts *(Ecological Linguistics)*
70 bitmap foreign fonts (Latin- and non-Latin-based) /
$50 per font / $35 per font for home use / 50%
surcharge per font for multiple users / extra charges for
modified system files, application files, and alphabetical
sorts

Fonts *(Judith Sutcliffe: The Electric Typographer)*
9 volumes, 15 calligraphic fonts / $45–$79.95 per volume

Foreign Fonts Edition *(Devonian International)*
22 multilingual fonts / $69.95 complete

MonsterFonts *(Showker)*
Shareware

Orchestra of Fonts *(Miles Computing)*
1 volume (Mac The Knife, Vol. 4), 30 fonts in 5 sizes /
$49.95

Works of Art Laser Fonts *(Springboard Software)*
5 fonts in 12 styles / $99.95 complete

World Class Fonts *(Dubl-Click)*
1: The Originals (71 fonts in 1–4 sizes / 2: The Stylish
(35 fonts in 1–6 sizes, some large) / 3: The Giants (19
fonts from volumes 1 and 2, in 1–6 large sizes) / 4: The
Triples (43 fonts suitable for ImageWriter LQ and
AppleFax modems, 2–6 sizes, some large) / $79.95 per
volume

PC—PCL Cartridges

AlphaJet *(Anacom)*
25 cartridges / $127.50–$212.50 per cartridge

AlphaJet Maxi-One *(Anacom)*
72 fonts in Roman-8 character sets, including barcode and
OCR / $545 complete

AlphaJet Maxi-Plus *(Anacom)*
40 fonts in ASCII and legal character sets / $225
complete

Everex A-to-Z *(Everex)*
230 fonts (50 portrait, 180 landscape) in many character
sets, including barcode and OCR / $695 complete

Everex HardFont Library *(Everex)*
B: $165 / F, T: $185 / Z: $195 / BST: $225 / LGL, SST:
$250 / All-in-1: $395

Headlines in a Cartridge *(Pacific Data)*
18 portrait fonts (Helvetica and Times) in 6 large sizes
(Roman-8 and ASCII character sets) / $399

HP Fonts *(Hewlett-Packard)*
25 cartridges

PCL: A page description
language developed by Hewlett-
Packard. PCL fonts are scalable
and are built with vector
graphics. They do not contain
resolution hints, although PCL
Level 5 provides another form
of enhanced resolution. PCL is
more versatile with text than
with graphics.

CARTRIDGE FONTS: Come in a
permanently configured plug-in
module for your laser printer.

HP-Compatible Font Cartridges *(Laser Connection)*
24 cartridges (A–Z, W1, S1, S2) / $195 per cartridge,
average / $115–$295 price range

JetWare *(Computer Peripherals)*
JetFonts (1 font) / JetFont 4-in-1 (4 word-processing
fonts) / SuperSet (150 fonts, 2 cartridges) / SuperSet
International (216 fonts, 3 cartridges) / $145 or $245
JetFont A-Y cartridges / $325 JetFont Z cartridge / $495
JetFont Z1A cartridge / $345 JetFont 4-in-1 / $445
SuperSet / $445 SuperSet International

Personalized Font Cartridges *(Innovative Type)*
15 type families, 2 barcodes, 2 OCR fonts / $225 256K
cartridge / $325 512K cartridge / $150 logos / $125
signatures / $20 modifications (per character)

Professional Collection Plus *(Laser Connection)*
65 fonts (56 portrait, 9 landscape) / $255 complete

Super Cartridges *(IQ Engineering)*
6 composite cartridges / Super Cartridge 1: 10 fonts /
Super Cartridge 1 Enhanced: 100 fonts / Super Cartridge
2: 17 fonts / Super Cartridge 2LC: selected landscape
complements for SC2 / Super Cartridge 2L: Complete
landscape complements for SC2 / $399 SC 1 / $599 SC 1
Enhanced / $699 SC 2 / $399 SC 2LC / $749 SC 2L

25 Cartridges in One *(Pacific Data)*
25 fonts in 12 character sets / $399

UDP Pro Collection Turbo Cartridge *(D. H. Systems)*
65 fonts (56 portrait, 9 landscape) in ASCII and legal
character sets / $249

PC—PCL SoftFonts

ACORN Plus SoftFonts *(Acorn Plus)*
15 volumes, 48 fonts / $150 per volume (4 fonts) /
$60–$250 price range

Architext Fonts *(Architext)*
200 fonts (Compugraphic, ITC, and proprietary) / prices
are for 1 printer/host / $150 catalog fonts
(portrait/landscape) / $495 catalog font sets / $300
progressions / $700 families / $50 Xerox 4045 cartridge
media

Atech Add-on Typefaces *(Atech)*
12 volumes proprietary fonts / 6 volumes Monotype fonts
/ $29.95 per volume, proprietary (2–3 fonts) / $79.95
per volume, Monotype (4 fonts)

CG/ITC Fonts *(VS Software)*
18 volumes, 75 fonts / $49.95 individual CG fonts by
point size / $59.95 individual ITC fonts by point size /
$169.95 Times/Triumvirate combo (36 fonts) / $219.95
Designer Collection (62 fonts) / $279.95 Executive Type
Classics (84 fonts) / $179.95 Headlines (45 fonts) /
$169.95 Ventura Supplemental FontPak (52 fonts)

Digi-Fonts! *(Digi-Duit!)*
33 volumes, 264 fonts / $49.95 per volume (8 fonts) /
$89.95 Basic Set (includes Digi-Duit! font generator and 8
fonts) / $399.95 Typeface Library / $20 DeskJet
Extension

FontMaker Fonts *(The Font Factory)*
14 volumes, faces licensed from AGFA Compugraphic,
ITC, Monotype / $194.95 per volume (4 fonts)

SOFT FONTS: Come on floppy disks. You can archive them in your computer or in your laser printer's RAM memory.

HP Fonts *(Hewlett-Packard)*
21 volumes / 5 combination volumes / HP also sells the
TypeDirector font and typeface management program
(under license from AGFA Compugraphic) / Premier
Collection: TypeDirector and 12 typefaces

LTI Softfonts Master Library *(LTI Softfonts International)*
200 fonts (100 portrait, 100 landscape) / $399.95
complete

MoreFonts *(MicroLogic Software)*
4 families (17 fonts, supporting 36 symbol sets) / $99.95
/ $49.95 each, additional families

SoftCraft PCL SoftFonts *(SoftCraft)*
50 Bitstream PCL font packages / $195 each

VSFonts *(VS Software)*
13 volumes (38 fonts, including math and Greek) /
$39.95 individual fonts by point size / $49.95–$159.95
by family / $200 custom 256K cartridge / $300 custom
512K cartridge

PC—Bitmap Soft Fonts

Diplomat Software Series *(VN Labs)*
Fonts for 35 foreign languages, priced per language /
$105 Basic FX Package / $165 NLQ Package / $165
LaserJet Package / $225 Laser/NLQ Package / $265
Ventura Package / $325 Laser/NLQ/Ventura Package /
$95 Fancy Font (SoftCraft) driver (laser and dot matrix
versions available) / $25 Keytop labels (4 languages
available) / $75 EGA/VGA screen font generator/loader

Fontasy *(ProSoft)*
38 volumes / $24.95 per volume (8–12 fonts)

HP Fonts *(Hewlett-Packard)*
21 volumes

KISS Family Fonts *(Laser Connection)*
17 volumes, 63 fonts

Laser Font Packs *(Eagle Systems)*
36 standard fonts, 8 specialty (licensed) fonts / $5 per
standard font / $15 per specialty or large size font / $99
per fontpack / 4 styles

LJFonts *(Weaver Graphics)*
143 fonts / $29.99 each

Office Series Fonts *(The Font Factory)*
18 volumes: HP cartridge font emulations / $69.95 each

SoftCraft Bitmap SoftFonts *(SoftCraft)*
12 Storch Premium Series bitmap font packages / 68
Softcraft bitmap fonts / $25 each, Storch font packages /
$15 each, SoftCraft fonts

CHAPTER TWO

Managing Your Fonts

Once you go beyond the fonts resident in your page layout software, drawing program, and/or laser printer, and purchase new fonts, you will need some way to control your font library effectively.

There are various ways to do it. Some programs concentrate on improving the quality of what you see on your screen. Others combine typefaces into families and make styles transparent on the font menu. You will also find downloaders, memory compressors, font ID conflict resolvers, font and keyboard mapping utilities, network servers, export filters, orientation converters (in the PCL environment), and font inventory reporters. Printer controllers also may contain one or more of these capabilities as subroutines.

To define font managers briefly, you can say that, as a group, they allow you to monitor, manage, and download your fonts.

Who benefits?

Macintosh users working with PostScript have a distinct advantage where font managers are concerned. Some Mac font managers are desk accessories. Others are INIT programs.

There are no font managers per se for the PC PostScript market. Hopefully this yawning abyss will disappear in the near future. However, there are more of these kinds of programs available for the PC PCL market than there are for PostScript on the Macintosh. Furthermore, these PCL font managers work with lots of page layout programs and laser printers.

Admittedly, the number of PCL font managers on the market also reflects the more restrictive nature of this document description language. There is more room for improvements.

Let's look at Macintosh utilities first.

Screen fonts

The hot new products in this department are the Adobe Type Manager (ATM) and TrueType (previously known as Royal Font) from Apple/MicroSoft. They create high-quality, scaled screen fonts by interrupting the command to generate them and creating them on the fly from the printer font outlines. This gives you a much sharper screen image than previous methods; it also eliminates the need to create and install multiple point sizes for screen fonts. FontSizer is another program that works in a similar fashion, and it is used by many manufacturers of font-related software as their screen font generator.

If you happen to be printing bitmap fonts rather than vector font outlines, the same utilities will give you much sharper output.

Many of the other font programs mentioned in this

INIT PROGRAMS: Automatically go into effect when you turn on your computer.

DESK ACCESSORIES: Utility programs that are called up from within other programs as needed.

Font/DA Juggler Plus offers users several powerful tools for font management in the Mac environment. The FontShow module gives an overall view of your library's status.

The FontList module includes both default font and reasonable facsimile versions.

FONT INVENTORY: Your type library.

DEFAULT FONT: The font your machine automatically starts up with.

FONT FAMILY: Different weights and styles (and sometimes character sets and orientations) of the same typeface. A well-rounded type library may contain upwards of 200 fonts, comprising 30 to 50 families. Ease of access is therefore an important consideration.

FAMILY BUILDING: Organization of your font library into intelligent groupings by typeface family.

book will no doubt support this new standard for screen fonts in the future.

Downloaders

Here is a list of some of the key features to look for in a downloader:
- Opens multiple files on multiple volumes.
- Allows downloadable fonts to be accessed outside the System Folder, even across a network.
- Compresses font data to minimize disk memory.
- Assigns a default font.
- Views current fonts, styles, and sizes.
- Prints a font or a list of fonts in any size and style combination.
- Switches from FONT to NFNT font identification numbers.
- Renames and renumbers fonts.
- Combines fonts into families.
- Makes styles transparent on the primary font menu.

Managing your font library

There are various programs that address the issues of font inventory, family building, and network support specifically, although these features are also found in some downloaders.

When it comes to font inventory, the ideal situation is to be able to create font tables and keyboard layouts for screen viewing or printed output. The ability to create customized reports is also essential. Font catalogues, sorts, style sheets, and summaries are some examples. In a sense, what you should be looking for here is the ability to perform database operations on your font resources.

You may want to create multiple versions of a single

font. Perhaps you routinely use a reduced character set for certain applications or multiple kerning tables for different point sizes. Some typographers not only kern text and display sizes differently, but also have separate kerning standards for specific clients. For example, a publisher who does children's books may request kerning within words, but no kerning around punctuation.

A well-thought-out font manager can make your basic font library much more versatile and easy to use.

Font management in the PC PCL environment

These PC programs tend to be more specific in aim than their Mac counterparts. Some are memory-resident (sometimes called terminate-and-stay-resident, or TSR) desk accessory equivalents, others are stand-alone programs.

In terms of screen fonts, the standard is basically whatever your page layout program will support, within the Windows or GEM operating environments.

PCL downloaders

PCL fonts come in many shapes and sizes. They can be resident in the printer or on cartridges or disks. Portrait and landscape orientations are considered entirely separate fonts.

There are many different standards in PCL font data structure. This means that the utilities only work with fonts from specific vendors. The kind of laser or inkjet printer is also critical. Generally speaking, you will have to buy specific import filters and printer drivers by name when ordering the product, because the font managers are driver- and printer-specific.

NETWORK SUPPORT: Managerial functions for the efficient use of fonts on a multiterminal system.

FONT TABLES: Another common term for font metrics.

KEYBOARD LAYOUTS: Alterable pathways between keyboard strokes and screen results.

Font/DA Utility allows you to rename, renumber, and reorder your fonts.

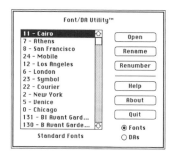

TSR Download, a soft font manager for the PCL market, controls both font downloading and printer commands. PCL font managers typically only show fonts in one default font format.

BackLoader is another PCL soft font downloader. This screen shows individual bitmap fonts and their memory requirements.

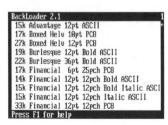

Some downloaders allow you to alter the size, color, contents, and position of the pop-up screens. Some use text-based, menu-driven approaches; others employ the what-you-see-is-what-you-get (WYSIWYG) approach.

Downloaders with the ability to convert back and forth between portrait and landscape orientation from the same font data will allow you to keep your PCL font library trim.

A full-featured PCL downloader offers many of the following features:

- Locates fonts and identifies them in English.
- Downloads fonts singly or in groups.
- Selects resident printer fonts.
- Displays names and memory requirements of all fonts currently resident in the printer.
- Displays RAM requirements of all fonts and warns if printer buffer is exceeded.
- Provides a printer control menu.
- Allows user-definable hot keys, color, screen position, and printer port.
- Operates in multiple soft font directories.
- Supports multiple character sets, orientations, and font formats.

Other issues

Both the Mac market and the PC market require certain features from a font manager that have little to do with the actual characters themselves. It is more a matter of organizing one's resources.

For example, being able to create and edit character sets is a plus that bears repeated emphasis. Memory management and printer command are equally important. Import and export filtering provide the necessary underpinning to make the system work. Touches like macros and a pleasing graphic user interface can make your font manager a treat to use. All these things must be considered when planning to buy.

Program compatibility is an important limitation to many font add-on products. However, with the publication of Adobe's Type 1 font secrets, many font product vendors are moving quickly to handle that format. Compatibility will become less of a problem as this feature becomes standard and costs also drop.

. . . .

Screen Environments

Adobe Type Manager *(Adobe Systems)*
For Macintosh / $99

TrueType *(Apple/Microsoft)*
For Macintosh

FaceLift *(Bitstream)*
For PC running Windows 3.0

Mac—PostScript

Family Builder *(Altsys)*
$100

Family Reunion *(Adobe)*
$65

Font/DA Juggler Plus *(ALSoft)*
$59.95

FontDisplay *(Jeffrey Shulman)*
$50

VTune is an add-on font manager for Ventura Publisher. The first screen shows the menu used to access different functions. The second screen shows the menu for spacing controls. The third screen shows the menu for custom creation of fractions.

This font table from FontDisplay, a Mac-based program, shows all available characters in a font and other pertinent information. The following four images were created with this program.

Font name: Garamond
Font size: 18 Others available: 10, 12, 14, 24
Font number: 14991
Location: Jeffs HD:System Folder:Fonts:"Fonts

	0	16	32	48	64	80	96	112	128	144	160	176	192	208	224	240
0			0	@	P	`	p	Ä	ê	†	∞	¿	–	‡	`
1		!	1	A	Q	a	q	Å	ë	°	±	¡	—	·	Ò
2		"	2	B	R	b	r	Ç	í	¢	≤	¬	"	,	Ú
3		#	3	C	S	c	s	É	ì	£	≥	√	"	„	Û
4		$	4	D	T	d	t	Ñ	î	§	¥	ƒ	'	‰	Ù
5		%	5	E	U	e	u	Ö	ï	•	μ	≈	'	Â	ı
6		&	6	F	V	f	v	Ü	ñ	¶	∂	Δ	÷	Ê	
7		'	7	G	W	g	w	á	ó	ß	Σ	·	◊	Á	
8		(	8	H	X	h	x	à	ò	®	Π	·	ÿ	Ë	
9		)	9	I	Y	i	y	â	ô	©	π	…	Ÿ	È	
10		*	:	J	Z	j	z	ã	ö	™	∫		⁄	Í	
11		+	;	K	[	k	{	å	õ	´	ª	À	¤	Î	
12		,	<	L	\	l	|	ç	ú	¨	º	Ã	‹	Ï	
13		-	=	M	]	m	}	é	ù	≠	Ω	Õ	›	Ì	
14		.	>	N	^	n	~	è	û	Æ	æ	Œ	fi	Ó	
15		/	?	O	_	o		ê	ü	Ø	ø	œ	fl	Ô	

The quick brown fox jumps over the lazy dog.

This key/caps table shows access keystrokes for each character in hex code format.

Font name: Zapf Dingbats
Font size: 14 Others available: 10, 12, 18, 24
Font number: 13 Chars Per Pica: 1.18
Location: Jeffs HD:System Folder:Fonts:"Fonts

FontShare *(TACTIC Software)*
$295

Master Juggler *(ALSoft)*
$89.95

Suitcase II *(Fifth Generation Systems)*
$79

PC—PCL

BackLoader *(Roxxolid)*
$89

ConoFonts Manager *(Conographic)*

Digi-install! *(Digi-Duit!)*
$20 per driver

ERMASOFT EasyFonts *(ERM Associates)*
$59.95

Font Library Manager *(VS Software)*
$79.95

JET:DESK *(Koch Software Industries)*
$95 / $1,995 multiple printer site license

LaserMenu *(MicroLogic Software)*
$99.95

TSRDownload *(Elfring Soft Fonts)*
$35 (specify HPDJ or HPLJ) / $35 utilities disk (specify HPDJ or HPLJ) / other packages with fonts available

TypeDirector *(AGFA Compugraphic)*
$225

Typographer *(Glyph Systems)*

WYSIfonts! *(SoftCraft)*
$95

These keyboard layouts show
access keystrokes for each
character in keyboard format.

Font name: Garamond
Font size: 14 Others available: 10, 12, 18, 24
Font number: 14991
Location: Jeffs HD:System Folder:Fonts:*Fonts

Normal

Shifted

Option

Option Shifted

The quick brown fox jumps over the lazy dog.

This font style sheet shows
sample output in each face and
style.

Font name: Garamond
Font size: 18 Others available: 10, 12, 14, 24
Font number: 14991
Location: Jeffs HD:System Folder:Fonts:*Fonts

Plain
abcdefghijklmnopqrstuvwxyz `1234567890-=[];',./\
ABCDEFGHIJKLMNOPQRSTUVWXYZ ~!@#$%^&*()_+[]:"<>?|

Italic
abcdefghijklmnopqrstuvwxyz `1234567890-=[];',./
ABCDEFGHIJKLMNOPQRSTUVWXYZ ~!@#$%^&()_+[]:"<>?|*

Underline Shadow
abcdefghijklmnopqrstuvwxyz `1234567890-=[];',./\
ABCDEFGHIJKLMNOPQRSTUVWXYZ ~!@#$%^&*()_+[]:"<
>?|

CHAPTER THREE

Editing Your Fonts

Typeface design has come a long way from the days of rubber molds and hot lead. Now the process is all done digitally, and you can do it yourself if you have the right tools.

Today's fonts are built from vector outlines and Bézier or Spline curves, with corresponding metrics and bitmap versions. Whereas the metal and film-master phototypesetting fonts of the past had characters that were fixed for all time, modern digital fonts are entirely open to modification.

Admittedly, typeface design can be a complicated and extremely time-consuming business. There are many conventions and subtleties totally beyond the average novice. Wholesale creation of new fonts is best left to the professional type foundries, but the ability to edit a few characters in a font is appealing, and the process can be quite easy.

The things you will most likely want to create with a font editor are special characters that may not have been included in the original font for one reason or another.

Examples include logos, fractions, ligatures, small caps, superiors and inferiors, old-style figures, swashes, and so on. But you may also want to change the shape of an existing character.

There are many different kinds of font editors for specific purposes, and there are also integrated programs that handle multiple operations.

Platforms

Several editors come in both Mac and PC versions. Most of the PostScript font editing software is concentrated in the Mac environment, but there are two excellent packages for PostScript on the PC platform too.

There is also a respectable showing of font editors for the PC PCL market. Some work specifically with fonts from one manufacturer (usually the same as the one that is selling the editor), but others are very versatile.

What font editors do

Here are some of the features to look for in this category of typographic tools for electronic publishing:

- Creates editable PostScript font outlines.
- Enables resolution hints and optical scaling.
- Produces outline printer fonts, bitmap screen fonts, kern pair tables, and other font metric data.
- Provides windows for font management, character editing, and font metrics.
- Draws characters freehand.
- Draws from templates.
- Reads and writes different font formats.
- Accesses soft fonts as well as printer-resident read-only memory (ROM) fonts.

VECTOR OUTLINES: Drawings based on combinations of straight lines, including tangents for curves.

BEZIER CURVES: Mathematically enhanced curves replacing tangents in vector outline type. Their secret lies in creating control points along a desired curve and then turning the straight vectors between them into mutually harmonious subcurves.

SPLINE CURVES: Another form of mathematically enhanced curves replacing tangents in vector outline type, but using a different mathematical formula than Bezier curves.

LIGATURES: Composite characters made of two (and sometimes three) elements. Examples include sp, st, fl, fi, ffi, ae, and oe.

SUPERIORS: Small figures that top-align with the cap height.

INFERIORS: Small figures that base-align with the baseline.

FONT FORMAT: The way in which an electronic font is built.

This screen shot shows a comparison between Type 3 screen fonts and Type 1 screen fonts using Adobe Type Manager. The program being used is Metamorphosis. This program is for upgrading your current Type 3 fonts to Type 1 format.

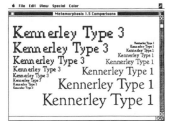

- Accesses scanned images for conversion into font format.
- Rotates images misaligned in the scanning process.

Briefly, font editors allow you to alter characters and retain the modified metrics. As in any other program for desktop publishing, a user-friendly interface with what-you-see-is-what-you-get (WYSIWYG) capability, zoom, good menus, and "undo" is a definite plus.

Some font-editing packages at the higher end of the price scale offer powerful font-tracking modules to assist you. Extensive typographic controls (such as the ability to support zero-width and overlapping characters), style sheets, global search and replace, and downloaders are several examples of these modules.

Font editors' split personalities

In fact, any font-editing package can contain up to three separate kinds of editors: screen font, printer font, and font metrics.

Bitmap screen font editors create editable bitmap images of characters on the screen, just as the name implies. You modify the character pixel by pixel. If you are using a font editor in which the screen and printer fonts are linked, then any change to one can be reflected in the other. The resulting screen font provides your visual reference to the PostScript outline version of the font destined for the printer. You can also alter your screen fonts for improved readability without affecting the printer fonts. However, not all screen font editors offer the option of acting on their printer counterparts.

Alternatively, you can print directly from your bitmap fonts to a non-PostScript laser printer (QuickDraw for the Mac, PCL for the PC).

Outline font editors work directly on the printer version of the font, and they usually create corresponding screen fonts automatically. Unless a product's sales literature specifically says that it works with fonts that are encrypted or contain resolution hints, assume that it does not.

PostScript outline font editors use five different approaches. Most font vendors support one or another of these font formats, but in the future, you can expect to see products that support all:

- Adobe Type 1 (with resolution hints).
- Adobe Type 3 (with no hints).
- Kingsley/ATF (with or without resolution hints and optical scaling).
- Monotype (with or without resolution hints).
- Digital Typeface Corporation (IKARUS format).
- TrueType (with or without hints).

PCL outline font editors operate under the Windows and/or GEM operating environments, or in the various font formats existing in PCL itself.

What's my line?

Font formats can be an extremely confusing aspect of desktop typography. A font's format is indicated by the three-letter extension following the name or code name of the typeface/style. The format is the key to host program and printer compatibility.

This confusing situation is not limited to fonts either. Graphics suffer from a vastly more complicated array of formats.

And that's not all. When editing fonts, you may find you wish to import a font from a graphics file. That font might exist in TIFF, Compressed TIFF, PICT, PCX, IMG, CDR, or another of more than thirty possible formats!

By the same token, you may be exporting your fonts to a drawing program that requires a particular format (such as Illustrator or Freehand).

FONTastic Plus is a bitmap font editor for the Mac environment. These three screens show a font management utility, a font table, and editing windows, respectively.

Sometimes, you may create a graphic with a draw or paint program and need to include it in a font, perhaps as a logo or special symbol. To do that, you need to find a font editor that can convert the format and to create the necessary corresponding font metric information.

Alternatively, you will need a graphics file conversion program to change the format into one your editor *can* handle.

Remember that when you alter a character with a drawing program, the resulting image is still just a picture. You cannot operate on it with a word processor or treat it like text at all, unless you take that additional step of creating font metrics and inserting it into a font.

Resolving resolution

Resolutions can vary widely between programs, and it is important to buy the product that will meet your needs. Some sales literature for PostScript font editors refer to resolution as dpi (300 is one example). Some talk about lines per em (8,000 and 15,000 being two examples). Generally speaking, PostScript editors are extremely precise.

PCL editors, on the other hand, can offer resolutions as low as 80 by 80 dpi (in one otherwise excellent program), or as high as 600 by 800 pixels (in another).

Granted, comparing dpi and pixels is a bit like comparing apples and oranges. Like the confusion between dots per inch and lines per inch, this bandying about of unrelatable numbers is sure to leave you with more questions than answers. Ask the vendors what their numbers mean, in terms you can understand.

Innumeracy is like illiteracy, except it affects our ability to understand and work with numbers. One example of how our mind tricks us: A 600-dpi laser printer has not twice the resolution of a 300-dpi machine, but four times as much. Three hundred dpi yields 90,000 dots per square inch. But 600 dpi yields 360,000 dots per square inch!

The editing palette

A good font editor will give you two layers behind the actual image you are working on: a template and a grid.

Graphics tools include universal operators and character-specific effects. Some of the former include condense, expand, independent or linked horizontal and vertical scaling, embolden, weight interpolation, rotate, flop, oblique, reverse, switch orientation (for PCL fonts), autotrace, and alter outline from control points.

The inclusion of tools for drawing lines, curves, circles, ellipses, boxes, fills, and so on is also a plus.

You will require the capability to copy, cut, paste, sort, group, and merge various character elements (such as strokes, ligatures, fractions, set widths, and other font metric data).

Look for the ability to support character substitution from other fonts (in PostScript, PCL, binary, octal, decimal, hexadecimal or ASCII format) and creation of reduced character sets for global search-and-replace adjustments.

Drive on

You will eventually want to output your new customized font. The final format of your font data will be determined by your operating system, desktop-publishing program environment, and laser printer or imagesetter.

If you are working in the Mac environment, you will generally have font format decisions that are simple to make. Getting it right in the PC environment is more complicated, although the end result can be every bit as perfect.

For PC PostScript, you need a font editor that will handle formats for Adobe PostScript (AFM), Windows (WFM), and/or GEM (GEM).

Fontographer is a very versatile font editor for the Mac environment. The following seven screen shots were created with this program. This screen shot shows the bitmap font-editing module.

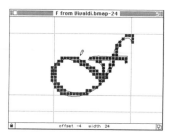

An auto-trace module allows you to create high-quality, editable Bezier outline versions from scanned bitmap font masters.

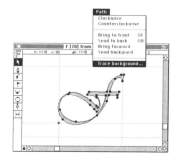

A metrics window allows you to control and view character width, spacing, offset, and kerning pairs.

Fontographer also includes a module for creating special effects.

Yet another module allows you to create composite characters.

For PC PCL, font formats are even more varied. The number of import filters you may require is greater. Some of the font extensions you may encounter are as follows:

- X45 (Xerox)
- BIT (Bitstream)
- WFM (Windows)
- GEM (GEM)
- FTX (Fontrix)
- HPR (cartridge fonts)
- PXL (T$_E$X)
- PFM (Pro-Font)
- Numerous graphic file formats

Conversion from one format to another is bidirectional in some instances, but only one-way in others.

You will also require export filters in certain situations, depending on your output device. Some of the typical format extensions you may require are LJP (Hewlett-Packard), CDS and LPX (Cordata), and AFF (AST).

Bells and whistles

Some vendors add to the appeal of their font editing products by adding peripheral features such as paint modules, kerning pair tables, and so on. You may find other stand-alone programs address these areas more effectively, but if you do not have those programs and do not plan to buy them in the near future, this option is worth considering.

Mac and PC—PostScript

ATF Type Designer I *(Kingsley/ATF)*
$449 with NFNT font format / $150 each, other font
formats / $1,000 optical scaling / $750 resolution hints /
additional license required for type foundries

MathType *(Design Science)*
$149

Mac—PostScript

ATF Typographer *(Kingsley/ATF)*
$595

FONTastic Plus *(Altsys)*
$99.95

FontLiner *(Taylored Graphics)*
$129.95

Fontographer *(Altsys)*
$495

FontSizer *(US Microlabs)*
$99.95

FontStudio *(Letraset)*
$595

Ikarus M *(Digital Typeface Corporation)*
$2,100 and up

JetLink Express *(GDT Softworks)*
$176 LaserWriter emulation / $234 LaserWriter Plus
emulation

You can also control fill
characteristics via the metrics
window.

Another module allows you to
design your own resolution
hints.

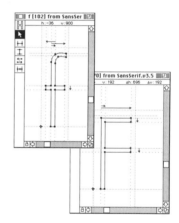

Publisher's Type Foundry, a font editor for the PC-PostScript market, includes both bitmap and outline-editing modules.

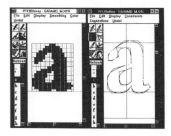

MathType is a Mac-based font editor for scientific applications. This screen shot shows a typical working situation.

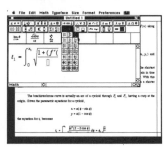

Metamorphosis *(Altsys)*
$295

ParaFont *(Design Science)*
$99

The Art Importer *(Altsys)*
$179

PC—PostScript

Publisher's Type Foundry *(Z-Soft)*
$495

SoftType *(Z-Soft)*
$199

PC—PCL

Digi-Duit! *(Digi-Duit!)*
$89.95 Basic Set (comes with 8 fonts)

FontGen V *(VS Software)*
$295

Font Solution Pack *(SoftCraft)*
$495

Glyphix *(SWFTE International)*
$79.95 installation kit (specify word processor) / $99.95 font sets, per volume

SoftCraft Font Editor *(SoftCraft)*
$290

CHAPTER FOUR

Font Effects

When you think of the font effects packages out there, you may see in your mind's eye an idealized sales brochure promising a program that will unleash the visual imagination and mesmerize your audience. But when typographers think about font effects, they see very specialized applications where effects are appropriate, and a temptingly well-paved road of good intentions.

What are font effects?

Bend, twist, distort, arch, stretch, flip, rotate, oblique, drop shadows, outlines, inlines, color breaks for spot color, separations for process color, shading, mirror image: it's a long list! Not every program offers every effect, but you can often buy expansion packs of additional effects, backgrounds, tints, and so on that will run under the program you have originally purchased.

You can also sometimes store formats as macros.

Some programs offer canned effects you can choose from a menu and then edit. With others you start from scratch. Some will allow you to combine effects but others will not. Some will give you a WYSIWYG display of your choices, some do not. Some preview to the screen in an uneditable form. Some text-based font effects programs only preview to the printer.

The ability to operate on clip art as well as type is sometimes a feature of font effects packages, as are collections of standard drawing tools.

Font effects versus draw programs

Once you start adding effects to a block of type, you are treating it as a picture rather than as a collection of words. Afterwards there is no going back.

As long as you are working with type as graphic, you may well wonder why you would not simply use a full-featured drawing program to do this sort of thing and benefit from many other inherent capabilities at the same time. You can ask yourself that question many times, without ever resolving it one way or the other. Programs specifically designed for font manipulation do have distinct advantages over draw programs, in spite of their limitations.

Straight from the can

For starters, most font effects programs are easy and fun to use. There is enough choice between products within both the Mac and PC PostScript markets, and the PC PCL market, to satisfy any quality and price calculations.

Picking options from the can be very intuitive. But unless the program combines the ability to work visually

You can do some amazing things with font effects. This sampling merely scratches the surface.

with a mouse and the ability to specify parameters with specific keystrokes, it can be limited in scope.

Resolutions and formats

There are basically two types of font effects programs, looked at from the point of view of output resolutions and formats: those that export encapsulated PostScript files (EPSF) and/or Illustrator files, and those that only handle PCL or bitmapped graphic file formats (such as PICT and Paint for Macs, or PCX and TIFF for PCs). You may also require the ability to embed EPSF files within PICT files.

The advent of the Adobe Type Manager has created a new market niche for PostScript font effects vendors. There is already one effects package designed specifically for that host program, and more will undoubtedly follow. Apple's TrueType will have a similar ripple effect.

Compatibility issues

As with other font add-ons, you should check to see that the particular program you are interested in supports the fonts you actually use. For example, most do not currently work with encrypted fonts. The ability to modify a diverse font library is important. Some packages come with a few fonts included, but not all. Look for products that have some good fonts from a reputable foundry as part of the package, if this is an important consideration for you.

There are other limitations too. Many of these programs do not allow you to combine effects—for example, a curve and a drop shadow.

Most do not permit you to modify individual characters in a text block—only the whole thing. Sometimes you cannot vary the font, size, or style within

Font effects can come well packaged and with lots of marketing savvy built into them.

the block either.

Effects programs generally work on the principle of frames. You change the frame and the type pours into it. Critical typographic refinements such as kerning, stroke fidelity, spacing of words and lines, and so on, can all be lost in that process.

At least one effects package allows you to create a randomly curved baseline and then pour type down it. (Some illustration programs refer to this as "text along a line.") However, most only allow you to modify existing lines of type.

For a program that is type-smart, you will have to pay more money.

When should you use effects?

Here is a list of the applications for font effects, in order of descending importance: presentation graphics, packaging, advertising, magazine wordmarks, magazine and newsletter headlines, brochures, books, corporate and technical documentation, and forms.

Resist the temptation to go wild. Success is not the same as excess. Use moderation; study the needs and expectations of your target audience first.

**The marvels of computer graphics can obscure the basic purpose of the news to inform....
Sophistication is not synonymous with understanding.**
R. Wurman

Mac and PC—PostScript

LaserOPTICS *(Linographics)*
Includes 28 modifiable effects / $495 Mac version / $595 PC version

Mac—PostScript

ClickArt Effects *(T/Maker)*
$49.95

LaserFX *(Postcraft International)*
30 modifiable effects / $195 / 6 expansion packs (each
with 10 effects and 5 background screens) / $49 per pack

LetraStudio *(Letraset)*
$495

SmartArt I, III and IV *(Emerald City Software)*
Each includes 15 modifiable effects / $149.95 per volume

TypeAlign *(Emerald City Software)*
$99.95

TypeStyler *(Broderbund)*
$199.95

PC—PostScript

Arts & Letters Graphics Composer *(Computer Support)*
$395 / $59–$129 for extra clip art libraries

Font Effects *(SoftCraft)*
$95

Font Special Effects Pack *(SoftCraft)*
$295

LPText *(London Pride)*
$99

Spinfont *(SoftCraft)*
$95

CHAPTER FIVE

Kerning

Remember one thing, right off. Kerning and tracking are absolutely essential ingredients in fine typography.

Creating effective kerning tables for your fonts is a thankless, picky, time-consuming burden, but it has to be done. Granted, readers got along fine with unkerned type and large letter spacing for hundreds of years. But today's discriminating readers have come to expect this enhancement. Properly spaced text is a joy to read.

It is unfortunate that many fonts feature well-cut characters but poor metrics. Kerning utilities help you to make up for that lack.

Mac users have a distinct advantage here over PC users because, while there is only one kerning package for PC PostScript, there are five for the Mac. There is also one PC PCL kerning utility, but it only works on fonts from the same vendor (who, admittedly, does have a fairly sizeable font catalogue).

Remember, too, that while kerning packages will help to automate the global kerning process, you will probably still need to perform manual kerning operations in many situations. Sometimes, the time and money required to create powerful automatic kerning resources is just not necessary, especially if your host application does not support kerning very well in the first place.

Kerning databases

Some kerning utilities provide you with ready-made pairs and values. Adobe fonts are supported in this way with roughly 100 kerning pairs. Bitstream fonts come with more than 500 kerning pairs. Additionally, leading DTP programs often offer very good kerning utilities as part of the package. The lack of good kerning resources should disappear as more vendors adopt the Adobe Type 1 standard. In some cases, you can only buy tables for a limited selection of fonts. In others, you can purchase tables for any or all existing and future Adobe PostScript fonts.

Some professional typographers have commented that font foundries have become much more sophisticated in their design of font metrics, eliminating the need for third-party tables. Enhancements such as zero- and fractional-width characters, overlapping characters, and sectored kerning can all be found in one or another font vendor's purchasing options.

The owner of one service bureau consulted with in researching this book explained that he had purchased a substantial number of kerning tables from one vendor and was very unhappy with them. He thought many of the character pair values were too tight. Unfortunately for him, it was not a global problem that could be handled with looser tracking. When he phoned the company, they told him that they designed the kerning tables with display point sizes in mind. They apologized for the fact that their product sometimes made body copy virtually unreadable, but explained that it was a trade-off: they chose to emphasize a different priority.

KernEdit is a benchmark-quality utility for the Mac environment. This screen shot shows many of its sophisticated and user-friendly features.

MacKern is another excellent kerning package. This screen shot shows why.

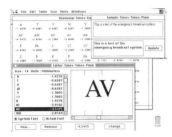

As mentioned earlier in this book, you may find you require two or three kerning tables for the same font, depending on how you plan to use it. So even if you buy kerning databases off the shelf, you will probably need a kerning editor to modify them or create new ones.

Kerning editors

Kerning editors may come bundled with kerning tables or as stand-alone programs. Basically, they allow you to go into the font metrics file and change things around. The main tasks your editor must perform are as follows:
- Read the font metric information.
- Display the information and changes on the screen.
- Make modifications to specific pairs.
- Save the changes.

The graphic interface

Kerning editors differ substantially in the way they present the information to you on the screen. Some give you much more information than others. The utilities that support high-definition screen fonts and working samples in larger point sizes are much more precise when it comes to visually respacing characters.

Features to look for

Which of the following features do you require?
- Pixel-by-pixel editing resolution.
- Unlimited pairs per font.
- Cut, copy, paste, sort, group, and merge of tables.
- Global tightening and loosening of tables.
- Filtering for specific character sets and point size ranges.

- Support for tracking (uniform white space reduction).
- Checking for font ID clashes, and conversion of fonts from FONT to NFNT format.
- Printing of samples.

Mac and PC—PostScript

LetrTuck + *(EDCO)*
Databases (24 volumes) and editor / $147 (specify Mac or PC) / $199 (Mac and PC versions together)

Mac—PostScript

KernData *(Pairs Software)*
Databases (69 volumes) / $70 per volume (4 fonts)

KernEdit *(Pairs Software)*
Editor / free with purchase of KernData

Kerningware *(Kerningware)*
Databases (35 volumes) and editor / $250 editor and LaserWriter Plus databases / $850 editor and databases for Adobe fonts to Vol. 39 / $1,050 editor and databases to Vol. 69 / $1,200 editor and databases for all present and future Adobe fonts

Kern-Rite *(The Software Shop)*
Editor / $195

MacKern *(ICOM Simulations)*
Editor / $195

PMtracker *(EDCO)*
Editor / $99

PC—PCL

Digi-Kern! *(Digi-Duit!)*
Databases (33 volumes) and editor / $39.95 complete

CHAPTER SIX

Templates

The role of the typographer in the publishing process is to provide coherent form to a written message. At the design level, this is called typographic design. At the input level, it is called coding.

Traditionally, one could save sets of codes as macros and apply them throughout a text fairly efficiently. The new electronic-publishing technologies have added a whole new dimension to coding by allowing code formats to be grouped together into one file that operates globally on other text files.

The way that page layout programs work gives us the ability to create complete grids before setting a single character.

Tag, you're it

The more typographic specifications you can include in your DTP page grid, the better off you are.

Many page layout programs allow you to create a style sheet for individual sections of your document, usually chapters. This is where all your type specifications reside.

The next step in the process is to import, or place, your text files. In order for things to come out the way you want, you must tag the different kinds of information in that text file, according to your style sheet.

Tagging systems can be crude or extremely powerful. At their simplest, they cover typeface, point size, style, leading, justification, and other basic typesetting parameters.

You should also consider tagging systems that allow you to indicate various levels of heads, running feet, tab structure (if any), tracking, and kerning.

The high-end standard for tagging is known as the Standard Generalized Mark-up Language (SGML). It is awesomely complete in its control over typographic refinements such as widow and orphan elimination, hyphenation reduction, page-length balancing, batch pagination, and so on.

TAG: A format command for copy that appears in the source data as delimited codes but in the output as the desired effect such as typographic specifications.

Canned goods

The truth of the matter is that, in spite of the benefits, creating and managing style sheets can quickly become an onerous chore, like making kerning tables.

This category of product enhancements for desktop typography offers you the opportunity to buy ready-made templates and style sheets for a wide variety of design situations.

There is quite a selection of packages in both the Mac and PC markets. In fact, PC users who run Ventura Publisher have the greatest choice of products. Users of PageMaker have the next largest pool of options, and there are several template packages for ReadySetGo as well.

Mix and match

Do you use any of the following publication formats on a regular basis? If so, template packages are an option you should seriously consider.
• Newsletters
• Tabloids
• Brochures
• Catalogues
• Business stationery
• Business documents
• Business forms
• Program management
• Time management
• Human resources management
• Sales and marketing management
• Charts and graphs
• Presentations
• Directories
• Technical documentation

Mix and match, part two

The number of design categories and the number of selections within them vary from vendor to vendor. In many cases, template designs for each kind of publishing need are sold separately and come with multiple elements. Sometimes, however, the product will include a more modest selection of options but for a wider range of applications.

A typical mixed package might include templates for 25 business documents, 15 newsletters, 15 corporate documents, and 10 technical documents. There are also templates designed specifically for formwork, and those products are listed in Chapter Eight, Formware.

The total number of templates or style sheets in a particular package averages about fifty.

The usual bells and whistles vendors include to get your business are on-line reference to page layout program manuals, illustrated glossaries of layout elements, booklets of numbered thumbnail sketches for each template in the package, and/or the ability to include nonprinting comments in style sheets.

You should also make sure that the templates are editable. Otherwise you will be locked into page and typesetting formats that do not necessarily fulfill your specific needs.

Templates of a different sort

There is another kind of template you may want to consider as a productivity enhancement: a graphics tablet.

This type of device replaces your pull-down menus and mouse with a touch-sensitive board that has a plastic overlay showing all the menu selections you normally see on your screen. There is also an area for sketching with a stylus.

Graphics tablets are popular in other related areas of computer-assisted design (CAD). A couple of manufacturers of these devices offer a Macintosh subtemplate for PageMaker, and/or PC subtemplates for Windows and PC PageMaker. Relatively speaking, compared to some desktop-publishing programs, graphics tablets are not very expensive. Some users find they speed up the page layout process by showing all menus at all times and eliminating repetitive mouse movements.

This graphics tablet has interactive overlays for various applications.

Graphics Tablets

Kurta Studio *(Kurta)*

MacMASTER and WinMASTER *(Promontory Systems)*
Graphics tablet / $195 master tablet / $195 each,
application templates

WIZ *(CalComp)*
Graphics tablet / $199 master tablet / $49 application
templates

Mac and PC—PostScript

Layouts *(Starburst Designs)*
219 templates (82 business, 35 letterhead, 48 envelope, 33
brochure, 14 newsletter, 5 flyer, 2 business card) /
$179.95

Page Designs Quick! *(PAR Publishing)*
120 templates / $139.95

Page Designs Quick! 5 *(PAR Publishing)*
225 templates / $284.95

PageMaker Portfolios *(Aldus)*
3 sets / $99 each

Mac—PostScript

Letraset Design Solution Templates *(Letraset)*
9 brochures / 6 newsletters / 9 catalogues / presentations
/ 50 business identity

Notes *(Layered)*
Guidelines and tips, 20 templates / $79

PC—PostScript

Document Gallery Style Sheets *(Micro Publishing)*
17 newsletters / 18 directories / 17 technical documents /
6 business forms / $39.95 per package

Style Sheets *(New Riders)*
30 business documents / 25 technical documents / 25
newsletters / $39.95 per package / $99.95 all three

Ventura Boulevard *(Computer Resources)*
21 style sheets / 21 chapter files / 7 templates/ $59.95
complete / $35 add-on index

Ventura Designer Stylesheets *(BCA/Desktop Designs)*
22 business documents / 11 newsletters / 13 corporate
documents / 10 technical documents / $149.95 per
package

CHAPTER SEVEN

Utilities

Shake hands with the wide world of electronic publishing. Utilities are your visa to visit the many diverse aspects of this complex process and understand the language in each of them.

This is the category of general-purpose toolboxes where we find programs that are eclectic, that do not fit into the previous chapters, or that are task-specific for unusual applications like music, multilingual hyphenation, pre-press assembly into signatures, import filters for word processing and database files, laser printer-to-plotter conversions, automated copyfitting and typographic specification, screen upgrades, style sheet editors, bar code generators, and optical character recognition systems.

That's a very mixed bag, but each one can help you dramatically in your desktop-publishing journey.

Music utilities

Typesetting music has always been a specialized field with few players (no pun intended). Desktop music publishing programs allow you to access musical instrument digital interface (MIDI) files for real-time transcription, page layout, and control of music fonts. Notation formats include orchestral, guitar, jazz/percussion, and MIDI data/events.

Finale *(Coda Music Software)*
Mac and PC / $1,000

Multilingual hyphenation

Getting it right is tough enough in English! But when you leave the familiar behind and reach out to a broader audience, much more can go wrong. At the very least, should you make mistakes in foreign language typesetting, your readers will think twice about taking your message seriously. At worst, you may create some colloquial faux pas that will leave you the laughing stock of your audience.

One particularly intractable difficulty in multilingual typesetting is keeping track of hyphenation rules that change from country to country. For example, Germanic languages using compound words have been immune to automated hyphenation until just recently.

Now you can buy hyphenation utilities for different languages that are 99 percent accurate, even with compound words.

Dashes *(Circle Noetic Services)*
Mac and PC / $95 per language

Pre-press assembly into signatures

The area of pre-press assembly into signatures may be electronic publishing's next quantum leap.

Impostrip is a powerful pre-press integrator that takes you beyond the horizon of individual pages into the world of multiple signatures. This screen shot shows the menu for basic signature parameters.

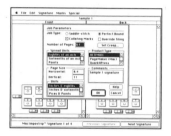

This screen shot shows print options, including tile, mock, scale, mirror, negative, marks, slug, colors, and printer size.

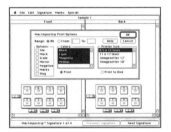

For many publishers, the laser printer is only a way station on the path to high-quality four-color offset printing. Most page layout programs and their related software peripherals do not give you the larger picture: signatures or page impositions that adjust for folding, binding, collating, saddle-stitch page creep, and multiple signatures for color separation.

Other pre-press tasks you will face include optional output to paper; negative or positive film or silver master plate; generation of proportionally reduced page proofs; tiling; mock-ups; scaling; cut, copy, paste, sort, group, and merge of signatures; mirror imaging; and negative imaging.

The purpose of pre-press programs is to assist you in this phase of the publishing process.

For the most part, pre-press programs come as modules in an integrated system. They can be very expensive. Although many vendors of high-end color separation systems (like Scitex, Crosfield, and Hell) support these pre-press functions, only one is included here, from a third-party vendor who does not manufacture color separation equipment. This is an extremely powerful program, yet it is probably of interest to a much wider audience than other, dedicated electronic pre-press pathways, and it is relatively inexpensive compared with other high-end pre-press utilities.

Unfortunately, space limitations do not permit expansion upon this subject in greater detail here. You will find much more information about the world of digital pre-press in other books and articles specifically on that subject.

Impostrip *(Ultimate Technographics)*
Mac and PC / $3,995 / $2,995 second copy / $9,995 service bureau version

Import filters for word-processing files

This category of utilities will interest you if you process a lot of text and require powerful import text-tagging features for SGML, TROFF, SQTROFF, GPO Bell Codes, XICS, and so on.

You will also find programs here that convert ASCII word-processing characters into true typographic coding for line returns, quotation marks, inch and foot marks, dashes, fixed and flexible spaces, fractions, special characters like copyright and trademark symbols, and so on.

dataTAG *(Publishing Solutions)*
PC / standard version $129.95 / typesetter's version $199.95 / SGML version $995

TagWrite *(Zandar)*
PC / $295

VTune *(ETI)*
PC Ventura Publisher add-on / $95

In certain cases which require use of a program to convert a specific word-processing format for the DTP system, the result could be single-direction workflow, making further editing on the word processor difficult or impossible.
J. Parnau

Import filters for database files

This category of utilities will interest you if you do a lot of database publishing. Database filters basically allow you to pour field-delimited text into your page layout without line-by-line formatting. For more options in database publishing, see Chapter Eight, Formware.

CopyFlow *(North Atlantic Publishing Systems)*
Mac Quark XTension / $395

DataShaper *(Benware)*
Mac / $149.95

FIELD DELIMITED: Data sorted into discrete categories called fields. These fields can contain numerous restraints on the type of data they will accept. They may also be active in the sense that they can evaluate and operate on their contents.

DataShaper is a database input filter for the Mac environment. It enables PageMaker users to draw upon database files of different kinds.

Synaptic PageLink *(Synaptic Electronic Publisher)*
Mac Quark XTension

Tycho *(Macreations)*
Mac / $149.95

Laser printer-to-plotter conversions

Sometimes you may want to run off your job with a plotter, vinyl cutter, scriber, or laser-cutting device, in one or another format. These programs let you do it with ease.

Interactive PostScript editors, macros, status reports, EPSF format creation, batch processing, and color support are features to look for, and the ability to interpret PostScript in native plotter language or vice versa.

PSPlot *(Legend Communications)*
PC / $105 / $155 with HPGL conversion option

QuikPlot.PS *(Taylored Graphics)*
PC / $250

Automated copyfitting

An automated copyfitting program will take the drudgery out of character-counting and copyfitting projections. The following utility is menu-driven.

AUTOCAST *(Autospec)*
PC / $395

Automated spec sheet generation

A program for automated spec sheet generation will create typographic specification sheets for bookwork in full or reduced laser printer formats. The following utility is editable with a word processor or from disk file via modem, and it supports SGML.

AUTOSPEC *(Autospec)*
PC / $475

Screen upgrades

Screen upgrade programs are currently limited primarily to use with Ventura Publisher. They enable video graphics array (VGA) and enhanced graphics adaptor (EGA) boards to store a full image of the page, allowing for page pans via mouse rather than scroll bar. In a sense, they allow you to emulate a virtual 19-inch full-page screen on a smaller monitor.

Additional drivers for various drawing programs running under Windows and GEM can also be purchased.

SoftKicker *(Aristocad)*
PC / standard version $99 / Plus version with additional drivers $139

Style sheet editors

Ventura Publisher users often have a specific need for powerful style sheet controls. A style sheet editor program has many.

File management features include display, print, copy, and delete of selected files, chapters, or publications. Documentation features include master catalogs for publications, chapters, and style sheets. Files can be accessed from the catalog regardless of location. Style sheet features include the ability to view and print tag descriptions, view chapters using different style sheets, view tag usage, print samples, and so on. With the enhanced version of the package, you can create database files (DBFs) containing your catalog entries and support global style sheet editing.

VP Toolbox *(System Network Architects)*
PC Ventura Publisher add-on / standard edition $99 / advanced edition $149

Odds and ends

There are a few other useful utilities that do not fit into any of the aforementioned categories. They include the following:

CorporateLadder *(BLOC Publishing)*
Chart designer / PC / $79.95

Dan Bricklin's PageGarden *(Software Garden)*
Laser printer controller / PC / $99

FontSpace *(Roxxolid)*
Font data compressor / PC–PCL / $89.95

Font Utilities I *(Budgetbytes)*
Public domain and shareware programs / Mac and PC / $3.19 per 400K disk

NYPPUG Test File *(New York Professional PostScript Users Group)*
Color PostScript sample output test files for equipment rating / Mac / $20

Publish by Design *(On Line Products)*
PC or Mac tutorial / $149.95

Publisher's PowerPak *(Atech)*
Font scaling and printer drivers / PC / $199.95 (specify
VP or WIN version)

Bar codes

Typesetting bar codes is a very specialized field, and it has
its own unique set of rules.

The bar codes themselves may wind up on packages,
forms, or labels, or incorporated into other kinds of
publications.

The use of these machine-readable messages is
increasing rapidly in our society, and many of the vendors
of bar code fonts and editors are also the same people
who sell bar code-reading equipment.

There are quite a few different kinds of bar code
symbologies: ISBN, EAN-8, EAN-13, UPC-A, UPC-E,
Interleaved 2 of 5, Code 39, and Postal, to mention the
most universally used. Some packages of bar code fonts
include few symbologies, but extensive variations and
controls. Others offer a wider selection of code formats
with fewer selections in each.

Features to look for in a bar code editor include
control magnification factor; rotation; human-readable
equivalents; batch processing; automatic incrementing and
decrementing of fields; file management; check digit
verification; error checking; graphics tools; appropriate
printer drivers; control of number of copies, paper travel,
left margin, and so on; support for multiple columns;
text-file input; and on-line help.

PostScript is a much more precise language than PCL
when it comes to creating bar codes. In the PCL
environment, bar codes are not scalable like text, without

significant data loss, especially on laser printers. You really need to output them on a high-resolution imagesetter if they are going to be small.

The only laser-printing alternative is to make them really big. That's fine if you are interested in bar codes for nonretail packaging labels and buy a stand-alone program designed specifically for that purpose. But if you are inserting bar codes into a page layout program with a desk accessory in the Mac environment or a memory-resident pop-up utility in the PC environment, small, razor-sharp bar codes with precise spacing are a must.

There are very many different bar code fonts and editors on the market to suit every user. Space does not permit a product listing here. Nevertheless, these points are worth mentioning because they give you a sense of what is involved in using bar codes in desktop typography.

Optical character recognition

Like bar coding, optical character recognition (OCR) is a field that is complex and expanding rapidly.

OCR has been around a while, but it was eclipsed for a time as a method for capturing data digitally by developments in modem and FAX communication. The OCR systems were quite limited at first in the number of fonts and formats they could read and write, so they were not very versatile.

But all that has changed. First of all, OCR technology took a quantum leap forward in its ability to accurately translate words from the printed medium into the electronic one. Nowadays it is often referred to as intelligent character recognition (ICR).

As an added thrust from an unexpected corner, the introduction of computer viruses has made electronic capture of other people's files a risky proposition. ICR offers one effective solution to this problem.

ICR systems can be very expensive, but some are moderately priced, considering the job they do. Some come bundled with a scanner, others do not. Some come bundled with other utilities as bells and whistles.

Features to look for in an ICR system include the ability to:

- Read and write typeset, proportionally-spaced, and kerned characters.
- Read and write underlined, bold, and italic fonts in various point sizes.
- Read and write justified, tabbed, indented, or bulleted text in portrait or landscape mode.
- Read and write various file formats such as EPSF, PICT, PCX, TIFF (including uncompressed bitmap, packbits, CCITT Group 3, and CCITT Group 4), ASCII (three kinds), Paint, DCA, RES, IGF, PDA, and so on.
- Compensate for character pitch and skew.
- Learn to read new fonts.
- Refer to a user-expandable dictionary.
- Differentiate columns.
- Control column ordering.
- Differentiate between text and graphics.
- Cut, copy and paste in text or graphics mode.
- Control halftone, bilevel, and gray scale for graphics mode.
- Handle multipage documents.
- Retain customized user settings.
- Read 40 to 150 characters per second (scanning speed).
- Scan and output at 300-dpi resolution or greater.
- Drive appropriate scanners.
- Avoid graphics, rules, and noise in text mode.
- Zone pages.
- Create alphanumeric recognition modes.
- Collate pages for duplex documents.

There are very many different ICR solutions on the market, incorporating different features. Space does not permit a product listing here, but these points are worth mentioning because they give you a sense of what is involved in using OCR and ICR in desktop typography. However, PC users have a much larger range of options available to them than Macintosh users.

Summing up your options

Expect to uncover problems in installing any DTP system, some of which you may be the first to discover, and not all of which can be resolved. You may have to compromise.
J. Parnau

So far, *Desktop Typographics* has dealt with products and programs for use with the page layout program you probably already have.

As you can see, there are many more fonts available than there are programs for typographic enhancement and typesetting process control.

In the next chapter, we are going to look at a range of products you may not be familiar with right now, but that will probably be a part of your desktop publishing future: formware.

But for now, let us sum up what has gone before.

Typesetting in any environment requires both high-quality imaging and powerful control of text. Typography in the desktop-publishing environment is fairly well developed where imaging is concerned. The enhancements described here can boost your management of text and typesetting specifications dramatically.

The picture is much more cloudy where documents include graphics and/or where page layout programs only represent one small node in a larger electronic pre-press workgroup. Not all of the products described in these chapters will support network applications.

CHAPTER EIGHT

Formware

Forms! The very word sends shivers down the collective spines of typographers and the form-filling public. But to the managers of corporate information, they are the lifeblood of daily operation.

For the desktop typographer, formwork falls into roughly two categories: design and completion. In larger, more powerful formware, these may be combined and other features may be offered such as sophisticated file management and database compatibility.

The many roles of form managers

Every electronic form management system will offer a different mix of features. Many offer different modules for different applications.

Typography, in the sense of beautiful fonts aesthetically spaced and positioned, is not one of the strong points of form programs. The type in forms does not have to adhere to the same high aesthetic standards we expect in other documents. Typesetting controls in some form design programs can be quite crude. Some form managers only work in ASCII. Others take advantage of the superior imaging capabilities of PostScript and PCL. Specialty fonts are also sometimes required to typeset forms, because some things like line-draw elements, charge card symbols, bar codes, and other unusual characters cannot be found on your average typeface.

One other thing the typographic design of forms requires is a very precise information hierarchy with many variables, particularly when the forms will be filled in electronically. For the typographer, this usually involves complex coding and formatting at the design stage. This sort of work involves mental arithmetic and working comments that do not appear in the final product.

Certain drawing requirements are universal in form design programs, such as the ability to create boxes, rounded corners, circles, ellipses, anamorphic objects, rules, combs, check boxes, tints, and so on. Some form design programs include the ability to import graphics in various file formats, and some vendors go so far as to offer digitization services to allow customers to include their company logos.

Last but not least, good formware must have the ability to process huge quantities of data in numerous field-delimited database formats.

Freedom of choice

There is more formware available than any other category of products for desktop typography except fonts—more vendors and more complete product lines. You are sure to find more than one package to meet your personal needs and budget, whether you are working on a Macintosh or a PC.

THREE DESIGN TIPS FOR PERFECT FORMS

1. The major difference between forms and other types of printed communication is that forms are designed to receive information rather than distribute it. Like other publications, they require careful planning and discussion before a single character or line is set.

2. Different types of information in a form may be desired from those who fill them in, may be destined for different people in your organization, or may require different kinds of action. Well-spaced logical groupings with clear captions, separated by lines, boxes, shading, and so on, can significantly improve information flow. Giving your form an attractive look and making it simple to fill in will inspire your respondents to participate.

3. Refining your forms is an ongoing process. In addition to proofreading, format checks, and modifications to contents and design, you must also test the database protocols you will use to process the information you receive. Testing the effectiveness of your forms in the field is also important.

A typical form design screen shot, taken from Informed Designer, a Mac-based program.

The complementary form filler screen shot, taken from Informed Mini-Manager.

In researching this book, the original assumption was that PostScript was the document description language of choice in all desktop-publishing applications. However, more familiarity with the market revealed that corporate publishing relied just as heavily on PCL, if not more so. The astounding number of PCL form programs, compared with PostScript ones, seems to substantiate this claim.

The overabundance of options makes it more difficult to describe how various kinds of form programs work, because they can work very differently indeed.

To make it easier, we will look at the topic from three angles: form design, form fill-in, and form management.

Form design

Here are some of the features you should look for in a well-rounded form design program:
- Menus for typeface, style, size, and justification.
- Menus for drawing objects.
- Cut, copy, paste, clear, duplicate, step-and-repeat, rotate, scale, sort, group, merge, and align form elements.
- WYSIWYG display.
- On-screen customizable rulers.
- Snap to grid, zoom, and undo.
- Support for bar codes.
- Support for spot color breaks, registration marks, and crop marks.
- Import filters for graphics files.
- Ability to import scanned forms as editable templates.
- Provision of ready-made form templates that you can customize.
- Ability to save and use form design elements as macros.
- Ability to create forms that can be filled in electronically.
- Ability to display two or more forms on the screen.

- Text editor.
- Working page for hidden calculations and comments.
- Ability to operate in a network.

Form fillers

Admittedly, form fillers are a little outside the generally accepted boundaries of typesetting in the desktop-publishing environment. But how forms are going to be filled in and managed has a direct impact on how they must be designed.

The long and the short of it is that forms, like spreadsheets and other database documents, work on the principle of fields. How you define them and combine them is critical. Unlike form designers, fillers do not necessarily require WYSIWYG screen displays, but some do operate in that way. Indeed, some fillers for the PC market come complete with run time versions of graphic environment shells such as Windows.

Form fillers and form managers sometimes overlap in their functionality, but for the purposes of this explanation, we will treat them separately.

Preparing your fields

Form design can be very repetitive. Certain kinds of information pop up in many different kinds of forms. The ability to automatically define field types in forms destined to be completed by computer helps speed up the process. For example, you may consider field data types for text, integers, decimals, dates, names, times, telephone numbers, and logical and captioned information.

Proper field definitions are the linchpins that make further form processing possible. There are even more considerations to resolve when it comes to formatting:

One benchmark database-publishing program in the PC-PostScript market, dbPublisher, offers excellent field definition and placement controls, as well as powerful database file access. Three different versions of the program are available: a standard edition, a professional edition for network installation, and a Ventura Publisher version.

For the most part, screens in database-publishing software demand a high level of literacy before you can feel comfortable with the workings of the programs. This screen shot illustrates how a powerful program often requires a great deal of familiarity before you understand what is going on.

Any piece of hardware or software that has to be described as user-friendly is probably not.
R. Wurman

choice lists; check lists; incrementing data; error checking; validation; text entry outside fields; locked fields; alphanumeric, alpha-only, and numeric-only fields; fields delimited by tabs, commas, periods, or lines; user-defined default values; and other field constraints.

Form fillers vary greatly in their ability to perform calculations on input data. Some products offer basic arithmetic. Others can handle more than one hundred kinds of complex math calculations (such as financial equations), if-then-else decisions, and Boolean logic.

Another fundamental division between classes of form fillers concerns printing. Some programs are designed to fill in only preprinted forms. Others allow you to save a form design as a printer macro and output the form and its data in a single pass.

Form management

The next step in the life of a form is integrating its information into the larger picture. This brings us to the whole subject of databases and database publishing.

When talking about form management, some typical verbs include *sort, group, merge, import,* and *export.* Each refers to specific tasks within the whole process. Sort, group, and merge are analogous to the cut, copy, and paste functions in the form creation process.

Basically, you want to be able to gather large quantities of information and manipulate them to give you additional insights. Thus we find form management is a critical part of accounting, taxation, inventory control, human resources, time management, and so on.

The way that form management programs and other database publishing programs actually fulfill the above goal is by working in tandem with relational databases of many kinds.

The ability of a form filler program to import existing data from diverse sources is extremely important. So is the ability to export its own data to other database formats, such as DBF, NDX, WKS, SYLK, comma-delimited, user-defined (UDF), and so on.

Another important feature in form management is "look up." Let's say, for example, you are working in the credit department of a large department store. Somebody calls you up and complains about a faulty product that was returned for credit, but the credit never made it onto the customer's monthly statement. You call the original complaint form onto your screen. Then you look up the customer's account information, directly from within the complaint form. These two bits of information may come from different directories in the store's host computer system. Hence the necessity for "look up" features in your form filler program.

Form management often requires the ability of its components to function in a network environment. Some form program vendors offer the option of purchasing additional form filler modules for use in distributed data-processing networks. Others sell site licenses.

Terminal emulation capabilities and communications utilities can also be included as part of the form management package.

It is important to remember that, when you are shopping for a form-design program, you are only buying the tip of the iceberg. There are many more issues to consider than just typesetting and drawing capabilities. What you want to do with your forms is a lot more important in many cases than how they look.

Database publishing

Any typographer will tell you that while forms may not constitute a large volume of day-to-day business, there are

As the following three images show, database publishing finds its home not only in the design, filling in, and management of electronic forms, but also in places as diverse as sales literature and parts catalogs.

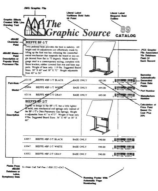

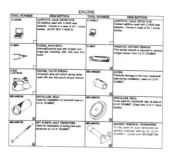

many instances where the same kind of mental arithmetic and formatting constraints can occur. Organizational charts, graphs, financial reports, directories, and business graphics of other kinds are a few examples.

In fact, there are also many other kinds of publishing that make use of database material.

Page layout programs vary markedly in their ability to handle these kinds of work. Third party software for database publishing is a rapidly growing field. Some products are stand-alone packages meant to replace or supplement your existing page layout program. Others are add-ons that work as part of the host page layout programs, accessible by menu, mouse, or keyboard in an interactive fashion. These enhancements often give you the power to go back and forth between your page layout program, databases, and spreadsheets.

Compatibility with larger mini- and mainframe computers with different operating environments, such as UNIX and VAX, and the abilities to print to numerous kinds of printers and handle a wide range of field-delimited data types may be important aspects of your personal desktop-publishing picture, even if you rarely work with forms.

Mac and PC—PostScript

FormSet *(Softview)*
$95

Mac—PostScript

FastForms *(Power Up Software)*
$149.95

FileMaker Pro *(Claris)*
$299

FLEXFORM Business Templates *(Antic Software)*
Forms templates for SmartForm Designer *(Claris)* /
Volume I: 42 templates (accounting and inventory) /
Volume II: 35 templates (administration and personnel) /
$69.95 per volume / $119.95 for both

INFORMED Designer, INFORMED Mini-Manager *(Shana)*
$295 Designer and one Mini-Manager filler module /
$195 each, additional Mini-Managers / $395 each,
4-pack of Mini-Managers

SmartForm Designer and SmartForm Assistant *(Claris)*
$399 Designer and one Assistant module / $49 each,
additional SmartForm Assistant filler modules / $399
10-pack of Assistants / $750 50-pack of Assistants

TrueForm *(Adobe Systems)*
$395

PC—PostScript

dbPublisher *(Digital Composition Systems)*
$495 / $695 network version

FormMaker *(FormMaker Software)*
$495 / $695 with 40 fonts / $395 FormEntry filler
module / $395 FormSpooler print spooler / $195
additional run time package

FormMaker's Horizon *(FormMaker Software)*
$195

PerFORM *(Delrina Technology)*
$295 / Pro version $495

PowerForm *(The Computer Group)*
$495

Xerox FormBase *(Ventura Software)*
$495

PC—PCL

FormEasy *(Graphics Development International)*
$495 / FormScan $595 / FormExpress $99

FormFiller *(BLOC Publishing)*
$149 filler only

FormGen II *(FormGen)*
$129 / Plus version $249

FormKits *(FormWorx)*
Forms templates for FormWorx with Fill & File /
Business (70) / Time Management (70) / Charts and
Graphs (112) / Personnel (70) / Project Management (70)
/ Sales and Marketing Management (70)

FormLab *(PYXEL Applications)*
$150

FormSet *(Orbit Enterprises)*
$189.95 designer only / II version with filler also
available

FormTool *(BLOC Publishing)*
 $95 designer only

FormWorx System 2 *(FormWorx)*
$299

FormWorx with Fill & File *(FormWorx)*
$149

JetForm *(Indigo Software)*
$495 CDN, JetForm-Design / $239 CDN, JetForm-Print
for Windows / $239 CDN, JetForm-Print for PC / $720
or $1,800 CDN (depending on host), JetForm-Merge

Lasersoft/Complete *(Business Systems International)*
$495 / $295 additional workstation entry modules

Lasersoft/PC *(Business Systems International)*
$375 designer only

CHAPTER NINE

Phototypesetter Drivers

You have successfully combined all the desktop-publishing skills and capabilities we have discussed so far. One last step remains to be taken: output.

For many desktop publishers, laser printers do not measure up as the output device of choice. They need phototypesetting.

Typographers, be they outside service bureaus or in-house company communications departments, may look to upgrade their existing equipment in order to handle jobs involving PostScript files, not to mention the many other kinds of digital input from telecommunication or media conversion. This category of products will be of interest to them.

Several vendors of typesetting equipment offer PCL support for particular models. But for the most part, PostScript compatibility has been the goal. Hence it is our subject here.

Even those who finish up with laser printer copies have considerable hurdles to overcome if they wish to use

PostScript on previously installed PCL laser printers, but that is the subject of Chapter Ten, PostScript Interpreters.

What are you driving?

There are a large number of third-party packages for driving phototypesetting machines with files from desktop applications. Mac and PC users all have lots to choose from. The more critical part of the equation is your particular typesetting machine and model.

What we are talking about here is not imagesetters with PostScript Raster Image Processors (RIPs). Rather, we are talking about programs that will take your text files (and graphics files, in some cases) and convert them into the proprietary, native operating language of your specific typesetting machine. That might be TTS, CORA, DENSY, or something else.

Here is a list of typical typesetting machines supported by one or another desktop driver:
- Alphatype 4900, 8900, and 9900; AlphaComposer (via Multiset III or WS III PC).
- Autologic APS-4 and APS-5; APS Micro-5 and APS-6; PIP.
- Compugraphic MCS; PowerView; Integrator; 8000, 8400, 8600, 9600, and 9700.
- Linotype CRTerminal; CRTronic 100, 101, 202N, 202W; Linotronic 300, 330, and 500.
- Varityper VT4300; Comp/Edit (all models 5410–6850); EPICS.

Degrees of usefulness

Some phototypesetter drivers are designed to output only text. But you cannot expect a DTP driver of this kind to exceed the capabilities of your typesetter. In other words,

it will not provide capabilities your typesetter does not
already offer, such as the power to rotate text, provide
previously unavailable point sizes, print in reverse or
flopped mode, and so on.

If you have an imagesetter that can handle graphics,
such a program will not do you the most good. One that
can at least retain copy positioning and leave blank panels
for graphics is a step in the right direction. Something that
can also give you the ability to print graphics is even
better.

Some vendors of typesetting machines offer special
graphic element fonts for graphics, allowing you more
control over rules, textures, shades, and so on. Certain of
the desktop drivers for typesetting machines allow you to
use your typesetter's graphics capabilities, but the
requirement for a specific graphic element font on-line is
not universal.

Most drivers simply give you the ability to access your
typesetting machine's fonts, font complements, and font
controls from within the DTP application. More
sophisticated packages also include the ability to
customize font width tables, alter font mapping, and
support kerning.

On-line, off-line

Conversions between desktop publishing files and
typesetting files can take place in two ways.

On one hand, you may be running your typesetting
machine in slave mode from your desktop-publishing
program. This is sometimes referred to as direct-connect.
In many cases, it can be done over a standard RS-232
cable, but some models of typesetting machines may
require another grade of cable and/or an interface box.
These small but crucial parts of the puzzle are often
available both from the manufacturer of the typesetter or

from the third-party driver vendor at competitive prices.

On the other hand, you may be converting the information off the production line, from disk to disk. This can work in two directions: translating DTP files into typesetter coding or bringing existing typesetter files into the desktop-publishing environment. It may involve handshaking with different kinds of front ends. Sometimes a program designed for this purpose will only work on certain models or product lines offered by a particular manufacturer.

The ability to convert and customize font metrics is a plus in this kind of driver too.

Most driver vendors sell drivers for both kinds of needs. Like drivers for direct-connect, drivers for disk-to-disk conversion are device-dependent and usually sold individually as modules.

Resolution

Of course, higher resolution is the main reason people look to phototypesetting for final output. Generally speaking, for text, DTP drivers will use your typesetter's highest resolution if you wish. But where graphics are involved, desktop drivers can sometimes be weak in taking advantage of the rated potential of your output device. Some packages will not accept Illustrator or EPSF files, for example, and other graphics may get set at low resolutions (less than 300 dpi in some products)—even when using a graphic element font.

Output speed is another factor. Some of these programs can be very slow, relatively speaking.

You may well consider purchasing a RIP that will allow you to output true PostScript on your typesetter. These are expensive, but fast and powerful.

Mac and PC—PostScript

Link *(Computer Solutions for Publishing)*
$1,990 with all PS-Links, T-Link for one typesetter, all
Link Utilities

Macintosh—PostScript

The Funnel *(The Computer Group)*

Macintize *(Mumford Micro Systems)*
CG MCS, PowerView, and Integrator to Mac / $995

MicroSetter II *(TeleTypesetting)*
$1,490 front-end version (requires telecommunication
capability in typesetter) / $1,800 front-end version with
TTS interface box / $2,500 slave version for
Compugraphic 8000, 8400 (requires Multiport serial
option) / $3,500 slave version for other machines

PageSet *(EDCO Services)*
$3,500

PostCode *(Mumford Micro Systems)*
$2,000

PC—PostScript

DAGRA/SET *(Davis Graphic Services)*
$2,390 ASCII version / $495 each, extra PageMaker and
Ventura Publisher drivers

microCOMPOSER Systems *(Cybertext)*
$2,295 microCOMPOSER / $495 microTYPE II
(includes microVISION with MCS microLASER) / $795
microTYPE III (includes microVISION with MCS
microLASER and microDISK) / Other modules are
available and may be required for your particular
application

MicroSetter-PS *(TeleTypesetting)*
$1,490 front-end version (requires telecommunication
capability in typesetter) / $1,800 front-end version with
TTS interface box / $2,500 slave version for
Compugraphic 8000 and 8400 (requires Multiport serial
option) / $3,500 slave version for other machines

One-for-All *(G.O. Graphics)*

PM/CORA and VP/CORA *(Xitron)*
$1,250 each

PubSet *(EDCO Services)*
$3,500

Typesetter's Connection: Ventura *(The Computer Group)*
$995 disk-conversion / $1,595 direct-connect (requires
standard MCS cable)

Typesetter's Connection: Windows *(The Computer
Group)*
$2,495

VepSet *(Mumford Micro Systems)*
$1,250 disk-to-disk version / $1,520 direct-connect
version (includes communications card and cable)

V-Prep 4.0 *(Parnau Graphics)*
$795

CHAPTER TEN

PostScript Interpreters

This chapter is about devices and programs that will allow you to output PostScript files on laser printers originally designed for PCL as a page description language.

There are basically two kinds of PostScript interpreters you can buy: programs that reside in the computer rather than the printer, and printer upgrade boards.

Macintosh users have a couple of products to choose from. But PC users have many more, because of the traditional link between PCs and PCL laser printers.

A question of interpretation?

The ability to produce different kinds of files is important: not only formats editable on a PC or a publishing system, but also print-image formats for output. An interactive PostScript editor is also a plus to look for in this kind of product.

The ability to handle many kinds of graphics file formats such as EPSF, TIFF, PICT, PICT2, PCX, and IMG, to name but a few, is something to look for too.

The current benchmark for PostScript interpreters is compatibility with PostScript version 47.0. The degree to which the products described here succeed in achieving this target varies in both quality and speed.

In fact, PostScript is rather more open-ended than might appear at first glance. Magazine write-in columns often feature shortcuts, debug routines, and so on that are not in Adobe's technical documentation for PostScript. Third-party vendors who seek to emulate the capabilities of this page description language can sometimes sacrifice speed or full functionality.

DEBUG: The process of correcting programming errors.

For example, some PostScript interpreters are not very user-friendly. Some do not support font scaling, rotation, or modification. Others are too slow to be of much use in a quick-paced production environment. Having a math coprocessor in your computer helps. So do extended or expanded memory boards and a large printer memory buffer. In fact, some packages require them if they are to work at all.

Fonts

Most packages come with resident fonts for your laser printer and allow you to access other downloaded fonts. However, support for Adobe Type 1 fonts is not yet universal. Some products will accept those fonts, others, only Adobe Type 3 fonts. Those that support fonts from other leading vendors (such as AGFA Compugraphic, Bitstream, Casady & Greene, Mactography, Monotype, and URW to mention a few) may or may not support Adobe fonts in any format.

Typically, thirteen fonts are supplied with the interpreter, to emulate the resident fonts from an Apple

Improving the quality of your laser printer output does not depend exclusively on system configuration. Sometimes it involves common sense. Three examples follow:
- Use a true bold-weight font rather than the "embolden" command.
- When setting type in reverse (white letters on a black or shaded background), use heavier weights of type.
- When setting color breaks, make sure registration is accurate.

LaserWriter on your PCL machine. Enhanced packages with equivalents to the thirty-five Apple LaserWriter Plus fonts are also available.

Printers

The range of printers you can use with PostScript interpreters is immense. Some vendors support more than forty laser, ink jet, dot matrix, and color thermal printers. Here is an abbreviated list:
- Epson FX, LX, and LQ printers.
- IBM Graphics and ProPrinter X24.
- Canon LBP-8II, CX and SX engines, and BJ-130.
- Hewlett-Packard LaserJet, LaserJet Plus, LaserJet Series II, Series IID, and Series III.
- Hewlett-Packard DeskJet and InkJet.
- Hewlett-Packard HP-GL plotters.
- NCR 6416.
- QMS color laser printers, KISS, BIG KISS, and SmartWriter.
- Ricoh 15EX and 6000EX, and Ricoh engines.
- Other printers that emulate one of the above.

Some PostScript interpreters in this category also have drivers for phototypesetting equipment.

The ability to handle all types of PostScript routines is sometimes decided by the capabilities of the printer rather than the interpreter. You must know whether both your interpreter and your printer can handle tasks such as text scaling, reverse type, circles, arcs, shading, patterns, rotation, stretching, clipping path, and so on.

CLIPPING PATH: Instructions for boundaries within which an image in one plane is superimposed on another image in the plane behind it.

The ability to switch back and forth between PostScript and PCL is also important. Some interpreters offer co-resident PCL emulation, but some only offer one option: PCL to PostScript.

Some products will support a local area network (LAN), but not all will. Some offer Micro Channel

Architecture for use with IBM PS/2 computers. Some can convert HP-GL files to EPSF format.

It also helps to find a product that is endorsed by the manufacturer of your laser printer. You can even sometimes buy third-party packages from that same manufacturer at competitive prices and with worthwhile guarantee safeguards.

Up against the boards

Printer upgrade boards are the hardware solution to PostScript interpretation. They usually involve one full-size board, not to be confused with your memory upgrade board. One excellent product, however, comes as a cartridge you plug in just as you would a font.

New PostScript interpreters seem to appear on the market on an almost weekly basis. It is a growth area. You can also expect numerous upgrades from vendors already in the field to support Adobe Type 1 fonts, now that Adobe has published their encryption secrets for licensing.

Purchasing a PCL laser printer with some sort of PostScript interpreter is now a very attractive alternative to a dedicated PostScript machine, in terms of price.

Interpreter vendors use the modular approach. Their products are device-specific. Many also sell memory upgrades for laser printers in 1-megabyte units. Two, 4 and 8 megabytes are common configurations that will help you achieve more on-line fonts, plus quicker processing and output.

PostScript development aids

There is another kind of PostScript utility you may require in your desktop-publishing situation: a PostScript editor.

Here are some of the features you can expect to find in these products:

- Text editor.
- Runnable glossary of PostScript routines.
- Graphics file format conversion.
- Ability to embed PostScript in other types of graphics file formats.
- PostScript dictionary.
- Detection of PostScript-routine errors.
- Ability to load, edit, preview, merge, and otherwise manipulate EPSF files.
- Provision of EPSF development tools.
- Ability to preview to Hercules, EGA, and VGA monitors.
- Ability to toggle between program text display and output graphics page display.
- Windowing into PostScript operand stack and graphics display.
- On-line descriptions of all PostScript operators.
- Generation of backgrounds, shading, rotation, clipping path, and all other PostScript functions.
- Provision of on-line resident fonts, and ability to work with downloaded fonts in many formats.

OPERAND STACK: The line-by-line instructions in the specific program application and data files you are running.

Mac and PC—Programs

PostScript Interpreter *(Shaffstall)*
$3,500 and up

Mac and PC—Upgrade Boards

Freedom of Press *(Custom Applications)*
$495

PSJet and PSJet-M *(QMS)*
$2,995 Mac version / $2,250 PC version

Macintosh—Programs

MacRIP PS *(TeleTypesetting)*

PostPrint *(TeleTypesetting)*
$99 with QuickDraw and HPLJ drivers / $295 each,
additional drivers

PC—Programs

GoScript *(LaserGo)*
$295 with 13 fonts / $539 with 35 fonts

Micrografx Enhanced PostScript Driver *(Micrografx)*
$199

UltraScript PC *(QMS)*
$195 / $495 Plus version with 47 resident fonts

PC—Upgrade Boards

ConoDesk 6000 *(Conographic)*
$2,395

EiconScript *(Eicon Technology)*
$2,795 PC version (for HPLJ and Canon LBP) / $2,995
PS/2 version (for HPLJ and Canon LBP) / $2,795 PC
version (for Ricoh) / $2,995 PS/2 version (for Ricoh) /
$650 memory upgrades per 1 megabyte / $395
EiconView module

JetScript *(QMS)*
$2,195

PacificPage *(Pacific Data Products)*
Cartridge format / $695

PageStyler II *(Destiny Technology)*

PC Publisher *(Imagen)*

PostCard *(Abaton)*
$3,495 / $1,795 Plus version

PS-388 *(Princeton Publishing Labs)*

RIPS Image 4000i *(Raster Image Processing Systems)*
$2,500 HPLJ, SX drivers / $2,600 Ricoh driver / $500
per extra megabyte of memory (up to 5 megabytes total)

Stellar PS *(Hanzon)*

POSTSCRIPT UTILITIES

Macintosh

Postility *(Postcraft International)*
$99

PostShow *(Lincoln & Co.)*
$224.95 with 13 fonts / $69.95 for 22 additional fonts

PC

PS Tutor *(Lincoln & Co.)*
$119.95 with 4 fonts (Roman style only) / $29.95 for 3
additional styles of each font / $69.95 for 22 additional
fonts (in 4 styles)

CHAPTER ELEVEN

File Managers

You have reached the last step in your electronic publishing odyssey, at least as far as desktop typography is concerned.

There are a few other programs available that do not really fit into the categories we have covered so far, but that can really help you to manage your DTP tasks with efficiency. Some are inexpensive, but more powerful managers cost quite a bit, relatively speaking.

Just like a service bureau

Here are a couple of products that can assist you in understanding the DTP process and controlling your document inventory.

Macintosh users are at a distinct disadvantage here, because the more powerful programs are built for the PC environment.

Basically, these programs offer you the ability to handle large quantities of documents, formats, and so on. Features to look for include the following:
• Support for telecommunication and disk conversion.
• Background operation.

- Batch processing.
- Printing and spooling options.
- Support for multiple printers, queues, and priority levels.
- Job recording.
- Automatic timed backup.
- Prep-file control.
- Provision of slug/banner page.
- Font management.
- Project management.
- Administrative function management.
- Financial management.
- Provision of management forms as editable templates.
- Database support.
- Inclusion of run time version of HyperCard.
- Graphic arts tutor.

The PC-to-Apple link

File management systems for DTP applications are particularly important in distributed workgroup offices. The ability to share information among machines is critical. TOPS and AppleTalk are two networks typically supported.

Various interested parties are trying to standardize PostScript and take control away from Adobe concerning what stays in, what comes out, and what gets added on to version 47.0. Should this come to pass, it will have some impact on what modules are available in file management systems. But for the most part, the real result of this proposed standardization will be felt in the PostScript interpreter category.

Mac

DTPAdvisor *(Broderbund)*
Includes tutorial / $79.95

PC

BureauMaster *(Compumation)*
$2,995

Desktop Manager *(New Riders)*
$99.95

PServe *(CoOperative Printing Solutions)*
$895 / $1,125 with AppleTalk Board (Daystar-PC) /
$1,195 with AppleTalk Board (Daystar-MCA)

CHAPTER TWELVE

Service Bureaus

What is a service bureau? Ask three different people, and you will probably get three different answers. They will all be correct.

Trade typographers who now handle DTP work are one kind of service bureau. Storefront operations that specialize in retail runoff of walk-in jobs are another kind. Electronic pre-press shops offering a wide range of imaging options are yet a third player in the service bureau marketplace.

In the preparation of this chapter, numerous typographers and two retail service bureaus were consulted.

The typical system

For the most part, service bureaus work in a Macintosh environment. Some have the ability to import text and graphics files from PC formats. This is not to say, however, that you cannot do everything well with a PC-based system. Many personally prefer the PC approach.

When you visit a service bureau, you can expect to find dedicated typesetting front-end terminals, microcomputers with extended or expanded memory, a large hard disk, and libraries of page layout and drawing programs as well as fonts, network software, a laser printer, and one or more phototypesetting machines with state-of-the-art PostScript RIPs.

Some companies offer a wide range of publishing aids from FAX to photocopies. Here is a list of possible tasks your service bureau might perform for you:

- Color keys
- Color separations
- Color proofs
- Computer graphics
- Consulting
- Database publishing
- Data conversions and processing
- Foreign language typesetting
- Forms
- Illustration
- Mathematical and scientific typesetting
- Mechanicals
- Modifications
- Overhead transparencies
- Photocopies
- Photography
- Photostats
- Presentation graphics
- Printing (Diazo, flexographic, offset, silkscreen)
- Run off (to line printer, laser printer, plotter, phototypesetter)
- Transfer type
- Translation

Companies which make the most specific, limited use of DTP tend to be those who are having the most success with it, and are the most happy with it.
J. Parnau

Time and money

Typographers who handle DTP work generally turn work around in twenty-four hours, as they do with conventional typesetting jobs. A common rate among type shops is $60 per hour, although small new companies may charge less, and large plants with sophisticated systems may charge more.

DTP work can also be charged out on a per-page basis. Some companies offer high-resolution output from a phototypesetter for as little as $6 a page. Much more common and realistic, however, is $12 to $15 per page.

These figures can sometimes be misleading. For example, if you request the bureau to go in and edit your DTP files, you will usually be charged for this service on an hourly basis, on top of the base rate.

Furthermore, running off a simple page of text takes much less time than running off a complex design with multiple graphic elements. Something like that can tie up a phototypesetter for hours, even if it has a state-of-the-art RIP. You cannot expect the shop to charge you the standard per-page rate in that situation.

Can you handle this?

In interviews with service bureau principals, it was mentioned that, in addition to page layout programs and fonts, there are many other programs that may have been used in the creation of a DTP document they might receive for output. They were asked what happened when that kind of job came into the shop.

The first thing everyone replied was that, for the most part, they either create the document from scratch (perhaps with digital data capture for input) or simply run it off for a set fee. Editing of other people's files is not a common practice, it would seem.

Another proviso that popped up in the interviews was that most service bureaus support a limited range of programs. For example, virtually all service bureaus operate only in PostScript, not PCL, as opposed to corporate communications departments that fulfill similar functions.

Of course, different service bureaus have favorites when it comes to page layout and draw programs. But one other surprising thing discovered was that many only use Adobe fonts, and they cannot or will not take on jobs that use typefaces from other vendors.

In addition, many of the enhancements discussed in this book were completely new to most of the people talked with. They certainly did not have those particular programs or capabilities in their shops.

If you go to typographers and ask them to provide you with value-added services on your DTP files, they may tell you either to let them redo the job from the beginning or to forget it, because they do not have the programs or editing capability it would require.

Similarly, in a retail-oriented service bureau, you cannot expect to sit down on a terminal you are renting by the hour and create a document with all of the attributes and power that the programs and products described in this book could provide. The service bureau typically will not have the necessary software or equipment.

Will that be cash or charge card?

Being a retail desktop-publishing service bureau brings a particular kind of business philosophy and operating style with it. For one thing, it could involve extended hours when the shop is open to the public. Walk-in trade is a large part of the business, and customers may remain on-site for hours, with ongoing questions for staff.

Counterpersons may be young and inexperienced. They may know very little about typography, the larger world of electronic pre-press, the graphic arts, or printing. They should at least have a strong background in computing.

One graphic designer interviewed for this book recently made the switch to desktop publishing. Now she spends evenings and Saturdays down at the service bureau, knocking off her jobs. She likes the way DTP technology works, but she regrets the time spent away from her home and family. "I'd rather drop it off and leave it for someone else to do," she says.

What bugs you?

VIRUSES: Destructive, hidden programs in uploaded files that can wreak havoc on your computer system.

All of the service bureau people interviewed in researching this book said they routinely run virus checks on every disk or telecommunicated file they get.

Even so, mysterious glitches can still occur. Jobs that will run on one machine will not run on another. Registration for high-resolution color separations off a phototypesetter can be incorrect. Graphics can come out as blank gray panels.

Up until not too long ago, font ID clashes were a big problem for clients working with service bureaus. Simply put, if you used one generation of font format (such as FONT) to create a job and the service bureau used another (such as NFNT or a different FONT numbering system), you might get your work back set in the wrong face and with horrible spacing to boot.

When service bureau people were asked whether they ever broke their rule of no editing on run-off jobs, particularly when the client supplied their own fonts, their typical reply was, "Of course we can do it, but most of the time we do not. We like to work with our own fonts. We do not want any license infringement problems that could come from using someone else's fonts. Even though some unscrupulous types might be tempted to make copies of fonts for their own use, we do not. Besides, even when they send us the fonts, we do not necessarily have the ability to work with the font metrics. It is better to plan for typographic fine tuning beforehand rather than after the fact."

Here we go again

The one most important piece of advice for working with service bureaus is that you should expect the same level of professionalism from them that you would from any other typesetting, graphic arts, or pre-press establishment.

Look for companies with proven track records, knowledgeable and attentive staffs, and equipment compatible with your needs.

Where type is concerned, you can ask specifically whether they adhere to the Typographic Industry Terms and Conditions of Sale. This set of trade customs, or ethical guidelines, is published jointly by the Advertising Typographers Association, The National Composition and Pre-press Association, and the Typographers International Association. It covers many potentially contentious issues in both the conventional and electronic environments. A copy is included as an appendix to this book.

DTP systems have certain advantages over conventional systems but only in certain cases. The opposite is true in other cases.
J. Parnau

Respect the editing cycle

Do not expect instant results from your relationship with a service bureau. Take the time and effort required to create a solid working relationship. Jobs that repeat with the same format and different content over a long period are the most suited to success.

Remember too, that the editing process is a human cycle. It applies to desktop publishing just as much as to conventional typesetting. In fact, if anything, the possibility of making changes late in the game may even tempt you to extend your editing cycle.

You can expect to go through galley proofs, illustration proofs, page proofs, and final art.

A clear sense of objectives when designing and creating your document in the first place will eliminate many of the problems you could encounter later on. As one old typographer's proverb goes: The change that costs $1 at the keyboarding level costs $10 afterwards. Once the job has been assembled into final art, the same change could cost more than $100.

Graphics and service bureaus

In one sense, the problem is not really type at all: it is graphics. When service bureau owners were asked what sorts of problems they encountered in running off other people's DTP files, most of the scenarios they recounted involved images imported into page layout programs from draw packages and scanners.

For example, the client might not include the original graphics file. The result, depending on the particular page layout program and the size of the graphic, might be a system crash, no graphic, or a low-resolution bitmap version.

Alternatively, if color separations are required, the registration may be off. In situations where keylines and fill patterns abut, there may be no compensation for ink spread. Halftones can create numerous problems involving dot density, dithering, and so on.

A plea for tradition

Not every job is suited to desktop publishing. Sometimes, conventional typesetting and illustration, a drafting table, and your basic layout tools (knife, waxer, roller, and a clean cloth) are all that is really needed.

Vendors of desktop-publishing equipment and software would like you to believe this is not so. In truth, traditional layout is a very satisfying craft. Some people may not want to spend their working lives anchored in front of a video display terminal, thank you very much.

A service bureau that can offer you hands-on conventional layout may be more to your liking than one offering photocopies, a FAX service, instant printing, or other after-the-fact benefits. Similarly, you may prefer to perform this stage in the publishing process yourself, in the traditional manner. There is nothing wrong with that decision.

The last word

We have covered a lot of ground on our journey of exploration into type in the desktop-publishing environment. The appendixes that follow contain a wide range of resources to help you learn more about this exciting field and find the right products and programs for your needs.

I wish you success in your communication objectives, and hope that this book has given you the critical overview and access to tools to accomplish them.

APPENDIXES

Professional Associations

Periodicals

Books

Vendors

Typographic Industry Terms
and Conditions of Sale

Professional
Associations

Alliance Typographique Internationale
A. Typ. I.
BP 611, Ch-4142
Munchenstein, Switzerland
011-41-61-46-8820

Boston Computer Society
BCS
1 Center Plaza
Boston, MA 02108
617-367-8080

Desktop Publishing Applications Association
DPAA
10737 Indian Head Highway
Fort Washington, MD 20744
301-292-0600

Graphic Arts Technical Foundation
GATF
4615 Forbes Avenue
Pittsburgh, PA 15213
412-621-6941

International Association of Business Communicators
IABC
870 Market Street, #940
San Francisco, CA 94102
415-433-3400

Macintosh Consultants Network
MCN
PO Box 309
Bellevue, WA 98009
206-453-2729

National Association of Desktop Publishers
NADP
Museum Wharf
300 Congress Street
Boston, MA 02210
617-426-2885

National Association of Printers and Lithographers
NAPL
780 Palisade Avenue
Teaneck, NJ 07666
201-342-0700

National Computer Graphics Association
NCGA
2722 Merrilee Drive, #200
Fairfax, VA 22031
703-698-9600

National Composition and Pre-press Association
NCPA
1730 North Lynn Street
Arlington, VA 22209
703-841-8165

New York Professional PostScript Users Group
NYPPUG
c/o JCH Typography
352 Park Avenue South
New York, NY 10010
212-532-4000

PageMaker Users Group
PMUG
c/o NADP
PO Box 1410
Boston, MA 02205-0855
617-426-2885 (NADP)

Southwest Association of Desktop Publishers
SWADTP
1208 West Brooks
Norman, OK 73069
405-360-5554

Standard Page Specification Association
SPSA
c/o Optronics
7 Stuart Road
Chelmsford, MA 01824
508-256-4511

Typographers International Association
TIA
2233 Wisconsin Avenue NW, #235
Washington, DC 20007
202-965-3400

Ventura Publisher Users Group
VPUG
7502 Aaron Place
San Jose, CA 95139
408-227-5030

Periodicals

You will learn more about design by studying the average newsstand than by reading a magazine which uses shock graphics in an attempt to teach design.

J. Parnau

ALDUS MAGAZINE
Aldus Corporation
411 First Avenue South
Seattle, WA 98104-2871
Bimonthly: 64 pages
$18 per year

BOVE & RHODES INSIDE REPORT ON DTP AND MULTIMEDIA
PO Box 1289
Gualala, CA 95445
Monthly: 12 pages
$195 per year ($220 foreign)

COLOPHON
Adobe Systems
PO Box 7900
Mountain View, CA 94039
Biannual tabloid: 16 pages
Free

DATAPRO REPORT ON ELECTRONIC PUBLISHING SYSTEMS
Datapro Research Corporation
600 Delran Parkway
Delran, NJ 08075
Monthly: 100 pages
$539 per year ($930 in Canada)
Subscription includes all back issues (approximately 900 pages)

THE DESKTOP
342 East Third Street
Loveland, CO 80537
Monthly
$87 per year

DESKTOP COMMUNICATIONS
48 East Forty-Third Street
New York, NY 10017
Bimonthly: 100 pages
$24 per year ($36 in Canada)

DESKTOP NEWSLETTER FOR ELECTRONIC PUBLISHERS
United Communications Group
4550 Montgomery Avenue, #700N
Bethesda, MD 20814
Monthly
$92 per year

DESKTOP PUBLISHING JOURNAL
4027-C Rucker Avenue, #821
Everett, WA 98201
Monthly

DESKTOP PUBLISHER
PO Box 3200
Maple Glen, PA 19002
Monthly tabloid: 28 pages
Free to qualified desktop publishers; $18 per year, others

DESKTOP PUBLISHERS' FORUM
National Association of Desktop Publishers
PO Box 508, Kenmore Station
Boston, MA 02215
Bimonthly: 8 pages
Free to NADP members; $95 per year, others

DESKTOP PUBLISHERS' JOURNAL
National Association of Desktop Publishers
PO Box 508, Kenmore Station
Boston, MA 02215
Quarterly: 144 pages
$60 per year ($80 in Canada)

DESKTOP PUBLISHING BUYER'S GUIDE
Bedford Communications
150 Fifth Avenue
New York, NY 10011
Quarterly
$54 per year

THE EDITORIAL EYE
Editorial Experts
66 Canal Center Plaza, #200
Alexandria, VA 22314
Monthly: 8 pages
$54 per year ($59 in Canada)

ELECTRONIC COMPOSITION & IMAGING
Youngblood Publishing
200 Yorkland Boulevard
Willowdale, ONT, Canada M2J 1R5
Bimonthly: 100 pages
$42 per year ($30 in Canada)

ELECTRONIC DIRECTIONS
23 East Fourth Street
New York, NY 10003
Quarterly
$30 per year

ELECTRONIC PUBLISHING
John Wiley
605 Third Avenue
New York, NY 10158
Quarterly
$155 per year

THE ELECTRONIC STUDIO
(insert in Studio Magazine)
Roger Murray & Associates
124 Galaxy Boulevard
Toronto, ONT, Canada M9W 4Y6
Bimonthly: 32 pages
$42 per year ($35 in Canada)

FONT & FUNCTION
Adobe Systems
PO Box 7900
Mountain View, CA 94039
Quarterly tabloid: 32 pages
Free

FORMS MAGAZINE
National Business Forms Association
433 East Monroe Avenue
Alexandria, VA 22301
Monthly
$24 per year

microPUBLISHING REPORT
21150 Hawthorne Boulevard, #104
Torrance, CA 90503
Monthly
$195 per year

THE PAGE
PO Box 14493, Dept. P
Chicago, IL 60614
10 issues per year
$55 per year

PC PUBLISHING
Hunter Publishing
950 Lee Street
Des Plaines, IL 60016
Monthly
$36 per year

PERSONAL COMPOSITION REPORT
Graphic Dimensions
134 Caversham Woods
Pittsford, NY 14534-2834
10 issues per year: 4 pages
$50 per year ($60 foreign)

PERSONAL PUBLISHING
Hitchcock Publishing
25W550 Geneva Road
Wheaton, IL 60188
Monthly: 100 pages
$24 per year

PRE-
South Wind Publishing
8340 Mission Road, #106
Prairie Village, KS 66206
Quarterly: 48 pages
Free to qualified persons; $16 per year, others ($32 in Canada)

PUBLISH!
PCW Communications
501 Second Street
San Francisco, CA 94107
Monthly: 100 pages
$39.90 per year ($54.90 in Canada)

PUBLISHING TECHNOLOGY
North American Publishing
401 North Broad Street
Philadelphia, PA 19108
Quarterly
Free to qualified publishers

THE SEYBOLD REPORT ON DESKTOP PUBLISHING
Seybold Publications
PO Box 644
Media, PA 19063
Monthly: 36 pages
$192 per year ($198 in Canada)

THE SEYBOLD REPORT ON PUBLISHING SYSTEMS
Seybold Publications
PO Box 644
Media, PA 19063
Biweekly: 48 pages
$288 per year ($300 in Canada)

STEP-BY-STEP ELECTRONIC DESIGN
Dynamic Graphics
6000 North Forest Park Drive
Peoria, IL 61614
Monthly: 16 pages
$48 per year ($57 in Canada)

TYPEWORLD
Typeworld Educational Association
PO Box 170
Salem, NH 03079
Biweekly tabloid: 32 pages
$30 per year

THE TYPOGRAPHER
Typographers International Association
2262 Hall Place NW
Washington, DC 20007
Bimonthly tabloid: 48 pages
Free to commercial typographers; $18 per year, others

TYPOGRAPHIC i
Typographers International Association
2262 Hall Place NW
Washington, DC 20007
Quarterly: 16 pages
Free from TIA member firms

UPPER & LOWER CASE (U&lc)
International Typeface Corporation
2 Hammarskjold Plaza
New York, NY 10017
Quarterly: 88 pages
Free to persons in the graphic arts; $10 per year, others
($15 foreign)

VENTURA PROFESSIONAL!
Ventura Publisher Users Group
7502 Aaron Place
San Jose, CA 95139
Monthly: 60 pages
$36 per year ($48 in Canada)

VERBUM
PO Box 15439
San Diego, CA 92115
Quarterly: 60 pages
$28 per year ($36 in Canada)

THE WEIGAND REPORT
Rae Productions International
PO Box 647
Gales Ferry, CT 06335
Semiquarterly: 16 pages
$65 per year

Books

Typography and typesetting

The ABCs of Typography
Sandra Ernst-Moriarty
New York: Art Direction Books, 1984

American Typography Today
Rob Carter
New York: Van Nostrand Reinhold, 1989

The Art of Typography
Martin Solomon
New York: Watson-Guptill, 1986

Better Type
Betty Binns
New York: Watson-Guptill, 1989

The Chicago Guide to Preparing Electronic Manuscripts
Chicago: University of Chicago Press, 1987

Computer Typesetting
John Negru
New York: Van Nostrand Reinhold, 1988

The Designer's Guide to Text Type
J. Callan King & T. Esposito
New York: Van Nostrand Reinhold, 1980

Designer's Guide to Typography 1990
Norfolk, NE: Step by Step Graphics, 1990

Designing With Type
James Craig
New York: Watson-Guptill, 1980

The Grid
Allen Hurlburt
New York: Van Nostrand Reinhold, 1982

How to Spec Type
Alex White
New York: Watson-Guptill, 1987

How to Start, Operate and Enjoy a Successful Typesetting Business
Tom Buhl
Santa Barbara, CA: Homefront Graphics, 1981

How to Typeset from a Word Processor
Ronald Labuz
New York: R.R. Bowker, 1984

The Illustrated Dictionary of Typographic Communication
Michael Kleper
Pittsford, NY: Graphic Dimensions, 1984

The Interface Data Book for Word Processing/Typesetting
Ronald Labuz with Paul Altimonte
New York: R.R. Bowker, 1984

The Modification of Letter-Forms
Stanley Hess
New York: Art Direction Books, 1981

Phototypesetting
James Craig
New York: Watson-Guptill, 1983

Publication Design
Roy Paul Nelson
Dubuque, IA: William C. Brown Co., 1983

Rookledge's International Typefinder
C. Perfect & G. Rookledge
London, England: Sarema Press, 1983

The Thames & Hudson Manual of Typography
Rauri McLean
New York: Thames & Hudson, 1980

Type & Image: The Language of Graphic Design
Philip Meggs
New York: Van Nostrand Reinhold, 1989

The Typencyclopedia
Frank Romano
New York: R.R. Bowker, 1984

Type Processing: The Word Processing/Typesetting Connection
Dean Lem
Los Angeles: Dean Lem Associates, 1986

Typographic Communications Today
Edward Gottschall
Cambridge, MA: MIT Press, 1989

Typographic Design
R. Carter, B. Day, & P. Meggs
New York: Van Nostrand Reinhold, 1985

Typography: Design for Newspapers
Rolf Rehe
Carmel, IN: Design Research International, 1985

Typography: How to Make It Most Legible
Rolf Rehe
Carmel, IN: Design Research International, 1984

Typography 10
Type Directors Club Annual
New York: Watson-Guptill, 1989

The World of Digital Typesetting
Jonathan Seybold
Media, PA: Seybold Publications, 1984

Desktop design

The Art of Desktop Publishing
T. Bove, C. Rhodes, & W. Thomas
New York: Bantam, 1987

The BMUG Type Book
R. Simon & R. Lettieri
Berkeley, CA: Berkeley Macintosh Users Group, 1989

The Complete Book of Desktop Publishing
Makuta & Lawrence
Radnor, PA: Compute!, 1986

Compute!'s Quick & Easy Guide to Desktop Publishing
Dan McNeill
Radnor, PA: Compute!, 1987

Designing for Desktop Publishing
John Miles
San Francisco: Chronicle Books, 1987

Desktop Design Power
R. Black
New York: Bantam, 1989

Desktop Publisher's Legal Handbook
Carbondale, IL: Nova Publishing, 1990

Desktop Publishing
Davis, Barry, & Wiesenberg
Homewood, IL: Dow Jones–Irwin, 1986

Desktop Publishing
F. Davis et al.
Homewood, IL: Dow Jones–Irwin, 1987

Desktop Publishing
J. Price & C. Schnabel
New York: Bantam, 1987

Desktop Publishing: A Primer for Printers
Gordon Graham & Thad McIlroy
Arcadia House, 1990

Desktop Publishing Bible
The Waite Group; James Stockford, Editor
Indianapolis, IN: Howard W. Sams & Co., 1988

Desktop Publishing from A to Z
Grant, Athanasopoulos, & Kutlin
Berkeley, CA: Osborne/McGraw Hill, 1986

Desktop Publishing: The Awful Truth
Jeffery Parnau
New Berlin, WI: Parnau Graphics, 1989

Desktop Publishing on the IBM PC & Compatibles
Kevin Strehlo
Glenview, IL: Scott, Foresman, 1987

Desktop Publishing: Producing Professional Publications
Benedict Kruse
Albany, NY: Delmar, 1989

Desktop Publishing Sourcebook: Fonts & Clip-Art
Jami Borman
Rocklin, CA: Prima Publishing & Communication, 1990

Desktop Publishing Type & Graphics
D. McClelland & C. Danuloff
San Diego, CA: Harcourt Brace Jovanovich, 1987

Graphic Design Cookbook
L. Koren & W. Meckler
San Francisco: Chronicle Books, 1989

Handbook of Desktop Publishing
John Sans
Plano, TX: Wordware, 1987

IBM Desktop Publishing
G. Lanyi & J. Barrett
Blue Ridge Summit, PA: Windcrest, 1989

The Illustrated Handbook of Desktop Publishing and Typesetting
Michael Kleper
Blue Ridge Summit, PA: TAB Books, 1987

Introduction to Desktop Publishing
David Hewson
San Francisco: Chronicle Books, 1988

Looking Good in Print: A Guide to Basic Design for Desktop Publishing
Roger Parker
Chapel Hill, NC: Ventana, 1988

The Macintosh Font Book
Erfert Fenton
Berkeley, CA: Peachpit, 1989

The Make-Over Book: 101 Design Solutions for Desktop Publishing
Roger Parker
Chapel Hill, NC: Ventana Press, 1989

Newsletters from the Desktop: Creating Effective Publications with Your Computer
Roger Parker
Chapel Hill, NC: Ventana Press, 1990

Ready-to-Use Layouts for Desktop Design
D. Collier & K. Floyd
Cincinnati, OH: North Light Books, 1989

Aldus PageMaker

Desktop Publishing Using PageMaker on the Apple Macintosh
Andrew Lucas
New York: Halstead Press, 1987

Desktop Publishing Using PageMaker on the IBM PC
Busche
Englewood Cliffs, NJ: Prentice-Hall, 1989

Desktop Publishing with PageMaker
T. Bove & C. Rhodes
New York: Wiley, 1987

Illustrated PageMaker 3.0 (PC version)
B. Lowery & P. Moore
Plano, TX: Wordware, 1989

The Insider's Guide to PageMaker 3.0 (PC version)
Rick Sullivan
Glenview, IL: Scott, Foresman, 1990

Newsletter Publishing with PageMaker, Macintosh Version
F. Davis & J. Barry
Homewood, IL: Dow Jones–Irwin, 1987

PageMaker 3.0 by Example
T. Webster & D. Webster
Redwood City, CA: M&T Books, 1989

The PageMaker 3.0 Companion (PC version)
D. McClelland & C. Danuloff
Homewood, IL: Dow Jones–Irwin, 1989

PageMaker 3.0 Problem-Solver (PC version)
William Sanders
Glenview, IL: Scott, Foresman, 1989

Personal Publishing with PC PageMaker
Terry Ulick
Indianapolis, IN: Howard Sams & Co., 1987

Type from the Desktop: Designing with Type and Your Computer
Clifford Burke
Chapel Hill, NC: Ventana Press, 1990

Using Aldus PageMaker 3.0
D. Kramer & R. Parker
New York: Bantam, 1988

Xerox Ventura Publisher

The ABCs of Ventura
R. Cowart & S. Cummings
Alameda, CA: Sybex, 1989

Desktop Publishing Primer with Ventura Publisher
Kathy Lang
Indianapolis, IN: Howard Sams & Co., 1988

The Easy Ventura Book
Rick Altman
Berkeley, CA: Peachpit, 1990

Hands-On Ventura 2.0
C. Wallia & L. Hart
Englewood Cliffs, NJ: Prentice-Hall, 1989

Learning Ventura Publisher
Rick Altman
Berkeley, CA: Peachpit, 1990

Style Sheets for Business
M. Lubow
Thousand Oaks, CA: New Riders, 1990

Style Sheets for Newsletters
M. Lubow & P. Pattison
Thousand Oaks, CA: New Riders, 1988

Style Sheets for Technical Documents
B. Canfield & C. Canty
Thousand Oaks, CA: New Riders, 1988

Using Ventura Publisher
D. Burns, S. Venit, & L. Mercer
Carmel, IN: Que, 1989

Ventura: The Complete Reference
M. Holt & R. Birmele
Berkeley, CA: Osborne/McGraw-Hill, 1989

Ventura Desktop Tips & Techniques
Robert Wolenick
Glenview, IL: Scott, Foresman, 1988

Ventura Instant Reference
Matthew Holz
Alameda, CA: Sybex, 1989

Ventura Power Tools
Rick Altman
Alameda, CA: Sybex, 1989

Ventura Publisher: A Creative Approach
Elizabeth McClure
Blue Ridge Summit, PA: Windcrest, 1990

Ventura Publisher: Tips, Tricks, & Traps
Schuyler & Lininger
Carmel, IN: Que, 1989

Ventura Publisher for the IBM PC
Richard Jantz
New York: Wiley, 1987

Ventura Publisher Problem-Solver
C. Eichlin & E. McClure
Blue Ridge Summit, PA: TAB Books, 1988

Ventura Publisher 2.0: Mastering Desktop Publishing
Richard Jantz
New York: Wiley, 1989

Ventura Tips & Tricks
Ted Nace
Berkeley, CA: Peachpit, 1989

Ventura Troubleshooting Guide
John Abraham
Plano, TX: Wordware, 1989

Ventura 2.0
Rob Krumm
Portland, OR: MIS Press, 1989

Xerox Ventura Publisher from the Screen to the Page
S. Stevens & J. Barry
Homewood, IL: Dow Jones–Irwin, 1989

Quark XPress

Desktop Typography with Quark XPress
Frank Romano
Blue Ridge Summit, PA: Windcrest, 1988

Quark XPress Tips
Rolling Hills Estates, CA: Quark, 1990

PostScript

Graphic Design with PostScript
Gerard Kunkel
Glenview, IL: Scott, Foresman, 1990

Inside PostScript: An Analysis of the PostScript Interpreter on Canon Printer Engines
Frank Braswell
Berkeley, CA: Peachpit, 1990

Learning PostScript: A Visual Approach
Ross Smith
Berkeley, CA: Peachpit, 1990

The PostScript Cookbook
Barry Thomas
New York: Van Nostrand Reinhold, 1989

PostScript Language Program Design
Adobe Systems
Reading, MA: Addison-Wesley, 1988

PostScript Language Reference Manual
Adobe Systems
Reading, MA: Addison-Wesley, 1985

PostScript Language Tutorial & Cookbook
Adobe Systems
Reading, MA: Addison-Wesley, 1985

The PostScript Programmer's Reference Guide
David Holzgang
Glenview, IL: Scott, Foresman, 1989

Real World PostScript: Techniques from PostScript Professionals
Stephen Roth, Editor
Reading, MA: Addison-Wesley, 1988

The SPS Programmer's Reference Guide
David Holzgang
Glenview, IL: Scott, Foresman, 1991

Understanding PostScript Programming
David Holzgang
Alameda, CA: Sybex, 1989

Laser printers

DeskJet Unlimited
Steve Cummings
Berkeley, CA: Peachpit, 1990

The HP LaserJet Printer Handbook
Alfred Poor
Homewood, IL: Dow Jones–Irwin, 1989

The HP LaserJet Series II Printer: Desktop Publishing
N. Goldenthal
Chesterland, OH: Weber Systems, 1987

The LaserJet Font Book
K. Pfeiffer & D. Will-Harris
Berkeley, CA: Peachpit, 1990

The LaserJet Handbook
S. Bennett & P. Randall
New York: Simon & Schuster, 1988

LaserJet IIP Essentials
M. Handa & J. Whitmore
Berkeley, CA: Peachpit, 1990

LaserJet Unlimited
T. Nace & M. Gardner
Berkeley, CA: Peachpit, 1988

Laser Printers: Programming HPs and compatibles
Timothy Perrin
Portland, OR: MIS Press, 1988

Vendors

AAA

Abaton Technology
48431 Milmont Drive
Freemont, CA 94538
415-683-2226
PostCard, PostCard Plus

Acorn Plus
4219 West Olive Avenue, #2011
Burbank, CA 91505
213-876-5237
Acorn Plus Soft Fonts

Adobe Systems
PO Box 7900
Mountain View, CA 94039-7900
415-961-4400
Adobe Fonts, Publishing Packs (I, II, III), Collectors Editions (I, II), Family Reunion, Adobe Type Manager, TrueForm

AGFA Compugraphic
90 Industrial Way
Wilmington, MA 01887
508-658-0200
AGFAType, cgType, TypeDirector

Allotype Typographics
1600 Packard Road, #5
Ann Arbor, MI 48104
313-663-1989
Allotype Fonts

Alphabets
PO Box 5448
Evanston, IL 60204-5448
708-328-2733
*A*1 Prospera, A*1 Egyptian fonts*

ALSoft
PO Box 927
Spring, TX 77383-0927
713-353-4090
Font/DA Juggler Plus, MasterJuggler

Altsys
720 Avenue F, #109
Plano, TX 75074
214-424-4888
Faces PostScript Fonts, Faces Bitmap Fonts, Family Builder, Fontastic Plus, Fontographer, Metamorphosis, The Art Importer

Anacom General
1335 South Claudina Street
Anaheim, CA 92805-6235
714-774-8080
AlphaJet Font Cartridges

Antic Software
544 Second Street
San Francisco, CA 94107
415-957-0886
FLEXFORM Business Templates

Architext
121 Interpark Boulevard, #1101
San Antonio, TX 78216
512-490-2240
Architext Fonts

Aristocad
1650 Centre Pointe Drive
Milpitas, CA 95035
408-946-2747
Soft Kicker, Soft Kicker Plus

Atech Software
629 South Rancho Santa Fe Road, #367
San Marcos, CA 92069
619-438-6883
Atech Add-on Typefaces, Publisher's Powerpak

Autospec
PO Box 1037
Pacific Grove, CA 93950
408-649-0890
AutoCast, AutoSpec

BBB

BCA/Desktop Designs
PO Box 2191
Walnut Creek, CA 94595
415-946-1716
Ventura Designer Stylesheets

Bell & Howell Quintar
360 Amapola Avenue
Torrance, CA 90501
213-320-5700
Q-Script

Bitstream
Athenaeum House
215 First Street
Cambridge, MA 02142
617-497-6222
*Bitstream SoftFonts for the Macintosh, FaceLift,
Fontware, MacFontware*

BLOC Publishing
800 Southwest Thirty-Seventh Avenue, #765
Coral Gables, FL 33134
305-445-0903
Corporate Ladder, FormFiller, FormTool

Broderbund Software
17 Paul Drive
San Rafael, CA 94903-2101
415-492-3200
TypeStyler, DTP Advisor

Budgetbytes
1647 Southwest Forty-First Street
Topeka, KS 66609
913-266-2200
Public domain fonts and font utilities

Business Systems International
20942 Osborne Street
Canoga Park, CA 91304
818-998-7227
Lasersoft/PC, Lasersoft/Complete

CCC

CalComp
800-456-8000
WIZ graphics tablet, WIZ light pen

Casady & Greene
PO Box 223779
Carmel, CA 93922
408-624-8716
Fluent Fonts, Fluent Laser Fonts

Casey's Page Mill
6528 South Oneida Court
Englewood, CO 80111
303-220-1463
Bullets & Boxes Font

Circle Noetic Services
5 Pine Knoll Drive
Mount Vernon, NH 03057
603-672-6151
Dashes

Claris
5201 Patrick Henry Drive, Box 58168
Santa Clara, CA 95052-8168
408-987-7000
SmartForm Designer, FileMaker Pro

Coda Music Software
1401 East Seventy-Ninth Street
Minneapolis, MN 55425-1126
612-854-1288
Music Fonts, Finale

Compumation
820 North University Drive
State College, PA 16803
814-238-2120
BureauMaster

The Computer Group
PO Box 163
Middleton, WI 53562
608-273-1803
PowerForm; Typesetter's Connection: Ventura;
Typesetter's Connection: Windows; The Funnel

Computer Peripherals
667 Rancho Conejo Boulevard
Newbury Park, CA 91320
805-499-5751
JetWare Cartridge Fonts

Computer Resources
PO Box 426
Livingston, CA 95334-0426
209-394-8188
Ventura Boulevard

Computer Solutions for Publishing
1613 Alabama Street
Huntington Beach, CA 92648
714-536-7008
Link

Computer Support
15926 Midway Road
Dallas, TX 75244
214-661-8960
Arts & Letters Graphics Composer

Conographic
16802 Aston Street
Irvine, CA 92714-4895
714-474-1188
ConoDesk 6000, ConoFonts, ConoFonts Manager

CoOperative Printing Solutions
1027 Sanfords Walk
Tucker, GA 30084
404-496-0864
PServe

Custom Applications
900 Technology Park Drive
Building 8, Billerica, MA 01821
508-667-8585
Freedom of Press

Cybertext
PO Box 3488
Ashland, OR 97520
503-482-0733
microCOMPOSER Systems

DDD

Data Transforms
616 Washington Street
Denver, CO 80203
303-832-1501
Fontrix, Printrix

Davis Graphic Services
113 Emmons Road
Lansing, NY 14482
607-533-4710
DAGRA/SET

Delrina Technology
1945 Leslie Street
Toronto, ONT, Canada M3B 2M3
416-441-3676
PerFORM

Design Science
6475-B East Pacific Coast Highway, #392
Long Beach, CA 90803
213-433-0685
MathType, ParaFont

Destiny Technology
300 Montague Expressway
Milpitas, CA 95035
408-262-9400
PageStyler II

Devonian International Software
PO Box 2351
Montclair, CA 91763
714-621-0973
FONTagenix, Foreign Fonts Edition, LASERgenix

D. H. Systems
1940 Cotner Avenue
Los Angeles, CA 90025
213-479-4477
UDP Pro Collection Turbo Cartridge Fonts

Digi-Duit!
528 Commons Drive
Golden, CO 80401
303-526-9435
Digi-Duit!, Digi-Fonts!, Digi-Install!, Digi-Kern!

Digital Composition Systems
1715 West Northern Avenue
Phoenix, AZ 85021
602-870-7667
dbPublisher

Digital Typeface Corporation
400 World Trade Boulevard
Boston, MA 02210
617-439-5348
Ikarus M, URW Fonts

Dubl-Click Software
9316 Deering Avenue
Chatsworth, CA 91311
818-700-9525
World Class Fonts, World Class Laser Type

EEE

Eagle Systems
PO Box 502
Moorpark, CA 93021
805-529-6992
Laser FontPacks

Ecological Linguistics
PO Box 15156
Washington, DC 20003
202-546-5862
Foreign Language Fonts

EDCO Services
12410 North Dale Mabry Highway
Tampa, FL 33618
813-962-7800
ChangeRight Professional, LetrTuck +, PageSet,
PMtracker, PubSet

Eicon Technology
2196 Twenty-Third Avenue
Montréal, QUE, Canada H8T 3H7
514-631-2592
EiconScript

18 + Fonts
337 White Hall Terrace
Bloomingdale, IL 60108
708-980-0887
QD Mac Fonts

Elfring Soft Fonts
PO Box 61
Wasco, IL 60183
708-377-3520
FontSpace, TSR Download

ElseWare
713 NE Northlake Way
Seattle, WA 98105
206-547-9623
DataShaper

EmDash
PO Box 8256
Northfield, IL 60093
708-441-6699
FontSets (I, II)

Emerald City Software
1040 Marsh Road, #110
Menlo Park, CA 94025
415-324-8080
Smart Art (I, II, III, IV), TypeAlign

ERM Associates
29015 Garden Oaks Court
Agoura Hills, CA 91301
818-707-3818
ERMASOFT EasyFonts

ETI Software
2930 Prospect Avenue
Cleveland, OH 44115-2108
216-241-1140
V Tune

Everex Systems
48431 Milmont Drive
Fremont, CA 94538
415-498-1111
Everex Cartridge Fonts

FFF

Fifth Generation Systems
11200 Industriplex Boulevard
Baton Rouge, LA 70809
504-291-7221
Suitcase II

The Font Factory
13601 Preston Road, #500W
Dallas, TX 75240
214-239-6085
FontMaker Fonts, Office Series Fonts

FormGen
64 Healey Road, #3
Bolton, ONT, Canada L7E 5A4
416-857-0022
FormGen II, FormGen Plus

FormMaker Software
111 Schillinger Road South
Mobile, AL 36608
205-633-3676
FormMaker, FormMaker's Horizon

FormWorx
1601 Trapelo Road
Waltham, MA 02154
617-890-4499
*FormKits, FormWorx System 2, FormWorx with Fill &
File*

GGG

GDT Softworks
4664 Lougheed Highway, #188
Burnaby, BC, Canada V5C 6B7
604-291-9121
JetLink Express

Giampa Textware
1340 East Pender Street
Vancouver, BC, Canada V5L 1V8
604-253-0815
Lanston Type Fonts

Glyph Systems
PO Box 134
Andover, MA 01810
508-470-1317
Typographer

G. O. Graphics
18 Ray Avenue
Burlington, MA 01803-4721
617-229-8900
One-For-All

Graphics Development International
20A Pimentel Court, Suite B
Novato, CA 94949
415-382-6600
FormEasy, FormScan, FormExpress

HHH

Hanzon
22032 Twenty-Third Drive Southeast
Bothell, WA 98021-4414
Stellar PS

Hewlett-Packard
4 Choke Cherry Road
Rockville, MD 20850
301-670-4300
HP Cartridge Fonts, HP SoftFonts, laser printers

III

ICOM Simulations
648 South Wheeling Road
Wheeling, IL 60090
708-520-4440
MacKern

Image Club Graphics
1902 Eleventh Street Southeast, #5
Calgary, ALTA, Canada T2G 3G2
403-262-8008
Typeface Library Fonts

Imagen
2650 San Tomas Expressway
Santa Clara, CA 95051
408-986-9400
PC Publisher PostScript Interpreter

Indigo Software
560 Rochester Street, #400
Ottawa, ONT, Canada K1S 5K2
613-594-3026
JetForm

Infotek
56 Camille
East Patchogue, NY 11772
516-289-9682
PostScript Interpreter

Innovative Type
13 Fairview Crescent
Groveland, MA 01834
508-372-7046
Personalized Cartridge Fonts

IQ Engineering
586 Weddell Drive
Sunnyvale, CA 94089
408-734-1161
Super Cartridge Fonts

JJJ

Judith Sutcliffe: The Electric Typographer
2216 Cliff Drive
Santa Barbara, CA 93109
805-966-7563
Fonts

KKK

Kerningware
61 Sorlyn Avenue
Toronto, ONT, Canada M6L 1H7
416-247-7976
Kerningware

Kingsley/ATF Type
2559-2 East Broadway
Tucson, AZ 85716
602-325-5884
ATF Classic Type, ATF Type Designer I, ATF Typographer

Koch Software Industries
11 West College Drive, Building C
Arlington Heights, IL 60004
708-398-5440
Jet:Desk

Kurta
3007 East Chambers
Phoenix, AZ 85040
602-276-5533
Kurta Studio

LLL

Laser Connection
7852 Schillinger Park West
Mobile, AL 36608
205-633-7223
HP-Compatible Cartridge Fonts, KISS Family Fonts,
Professional Collection Plus Cartridge Fonts

LaserGo
9235 Trade Place, Suite A
San Diego, CA 92126
619-530-2400
GoScript

Lasersmith
430 Martin Avenue
Santa Clara, CA 95050
408-727-7700
PostScript Interpreter

Layered
529 Main Street
Boston, MA 02129
617-242-7700
Notes for PageMaker

Legend Communications
54 Rosedale Avenue West
Brampton, ONT, Canada L6X 1K1
416-450-1010
PSPlot

Letraset USA
40 Eisenhower Drive
Paramus, NJ 07653
201-845-6100
*FontStudio, LetraFonts, LetraStudio, Letraset Design
Solution Templates*

Lincoln & Co.
29 Domino Drive
Concord, MA 01742
508-369-1441
PostShow, PS Tutor

Linguist's Software
PO Box 580
Edmonds, WA 98020-0580
206-775-1130
LaserFONTS

Linographics
770 North Main Street
Orange, CA 92668
714-639-0511
LaserOPTICS

Linotype
425 Oser Avenue
Hauppauge, NY 11788
516-434-2000
Linotype Fonts, imagesetters

London Pride
1 Birch Street
Norwalk, CT 06851
203-866-4806
LPText

LTI Softfonts International
14742 Beach Boulevard, #440
La Mirada, CA 90638
714-739-1453
LTI Softfonts Master Library

MMM

Macreations
329 Horizon Way
Pacifica, CA 94044
415-359-7649
Tycho

MacTography
326-D North Stonestreet Avenue
Rockville, MD 20850
301-424-3942
Fonts

Mephistopheles Systems
3629 Lankershim Boulevard
Hollywood, CA 90068
818-762-8150
MSDfont Sets, MSDfont SoftC Cartridge Equivalents,
MSDware

Merlin Publishing Group
2182 Kinridge Road
Marietta, GA 60032
404-973-0741
Fonts

Metro Software
2509 North Campbell Avenue, #214
Tucson, AZ 85719
602-292-0313
SuperFonts 25/1, LaserTwin

Micrografx
1303 Arapaho
Richardson, TX 75081-2444
214-234-1769
Micrografx Enhanced PostScript Driver

MicroLogic Software
6400 Hollis Street, #9
Emeryville, CA 94608
415-652-5464
LaserMenu

Micro Publishing
21150 Hawthorne Boulevard, #104
Torrance, CA 90503
213-371-5787
Document Gallery Style Sheets

Miles Computing
5115 Douglas Fir Road, Suite I
Calabasas, CA 91302
818-340-6300
Orchestra of Fonts (Mac the Knife, Vol. 1)

Monotype Typography USA
53 West Jackson Boulevard, #504
Chicago, IL 60604
312-855-1440
*Monotype Classic Type, Monotype Classic Type Expert
Sets*

Mumford Micro Systems
3933 Antone Road
Santa Barbara, CA 93110
805-687-5116
PostCode, VepSet

NNN

New Riders Publishing
31125 Via Colinas, #902
Westlake Village, CA 91362
818-991-5392
Desktop Manager, Style Sheets for Ventura Publisher

New York Professional PostScript Users Group
c/o JCH Typography
352 Park Avenue South
New York, NY 10010
212-532-4000
PostScript Color Test File

North Atlantic Publishing Systems
PO Box 682
Carlisle, MA 01741
508-250-8080
CopyFlow, CopyFlow Reports

OOO

On Line Products
20251 Century Boulevard
Germantown, MD 20874
301-428-3700
Publish by Design

Orbit Enterprises
PO Box 2875
Glen Ellyn, IL 60138
708-469-3405
FormSet, FormSet II

PPP

Pacific Data Products
9125 Rehco Road
San Diego, CA 92121
619-552-0880
Headlines in a Cartridge, 25 Cartridges in One,
PacificPage

Pacific Rim Data Sciences
3223 Mayberry Road
San Jose, CA 95127
415-651-7935
PostScript Interpreter

Page Studio Graphics
3175 North Price Road, #1050
Chandler, AZ 85224
602-839-2763
PIXymbols Fonts

Pairs Software
160 Vanderhoof Avenue, #201
Toronto, ONT, Canada M4G 4B8
416-421-9900
KernData, KernEdit

Paperback Software
2830 Ninth Street
Berkeley, CA 94710
415-644-2116
KeyCap Fonts

Par Publishing
6355 Topanga Canyon Boulevard, #307
Woodland Hills, CA 91367
818-340-8165
Page Designs Quick!, Page Designs Quick! 5

Parnau Graphics
PO Box 244
New Berlin, WI 53151
414-784-7252
V-Prep

Postcraft International
27811 Hopkins Avenue, #6
Valencia, CA 91355
805-257-1797
LaserFX, Postility

Power Up Software
2929 Campus Drive
San Mateo, CA 94403
415-345-5900
FastForms

Princeton Publishing Labs
19 Wall Street
Princeton, NJ 08540
609-924-1153
PS-388 PostScript Interpreter

Promontory Systems
1325 South 800 East
Orem, UT 84058
801-224-8833
MacMASTER, WinMASTER

ProSoft
7248 Bellaire Avenue
North Hollywood, CA 92025-0560
818-765-4444
Fontasy

Publishing Solutions
205 East Seventy-Eighth Street, #17T
New York, NY 10021
212-288-2470
dataTAG

Pyxel Applications
2917 Mohawk Drive
Richmond, VA 23235
804-320-5573
FormLab

QQQ

QMS
1 Magnum Pass
Mobile, AL 36618
205-633-4300
JetScript, PS Jet +, PS Jet + M, UltraScript PC

Quadram
1 Meca Way
Norcross, GA 30093
404-923-6666
PostScript Interpreter

RRR

Raster Image Processing Systems
4665 Nautilus Court South
Boulder, CO 80301
303-530-2910
RIPS Image 4000i

Roxxolid
3345 Vincent Road
Pleasant Hill, CA 94523-4318
415-256-0105
BackLoader, FontSpace

SSS

Shaffstall
7901 East Eighty-Eighth Street
Indianapolis, IN 46256
PostScript Interpreter

Shana
9650 Twentieth Avenue, #105
Edmonton, ALTA, Canada T6N 1G1
403-463-3330
INFORMED Designer, INFORMED Mini-Manager

Showker Graphic Arts & Design
15 Southgate
Harrisonburg, VA 22801
703-433-1527
MonsterFonts

Shulman, Jeffrey
PO Box 1218
Morgantown, WV 26507-1218
304-598-2090
FontDisplay

SoftCraft
16 North Carroll Street, #500
Madison, WI 53703
608-257-3300
Font Solution Pack, Font Special Effects Pack, SoftCraft Bitmap Soft Fonts, SoftCraft PCL Soft Fonts, SpinFont, WYSIfonts!

Softview
1721 Pacific Avenue, #100
Oxnard, CA 93033
805-385-5000
FormSet

Software Garden
PO Box 373
Newton Highlands, MA 02161
617-332-2240
Dan Bricklin's PageGarden

The Software Shop
233 Bedford Avenue
Bellmore, NY 11710
516-785-4147
Kern-Rite

Springboard Software
7808 Creekridge Circle
Minneapolis, MN 55435
612-944-3915
Works of Art Laser Fonts

Starburst Designs
1973 Nellis Boulevard, #315
Las Vegas, NV 89115
702-453-3371
Layouts

Studio 231
231 Bedford Avenue
Bellmore, NY 11710
516-785-4422
Studio231 Fonts

SWFTE International
128-D Senatorial Drive
Greenville, DE 19807
302-429-8434
Glyphix

Synaptic Electronic Publisher
1075 South Vandyke Road
Appleton, WI 54915
414-734-6535
Synaptic PageLink Quark XTension

System Network Architects
PO Box 3662
Princeton, NJ 08543
609-799-9605
VPToolbox

TTT

Tactic Software
13615 South Dixie Highway
Miami, FL 33176
305-378-4110
ArtFonts, FontShare

Taylored Graphics
PO Box 1900
Freedom, CA 95019-1900
408-761-2481
FontLiner, QuickPlot.PS

Teletypesetting
474 Commonwealth Avenue
Boston, MA 02215
617-266-6637
MacRIP, MicroSetter II, MicroSetter PS, PostPrint

T/Maker
1390 Villa Street
Mountain View, CA 94041
415-962-0195
*ClickArt Effects, ClickArt LaserLetters, ClickArt Letters
(I, II)*

Treacyfaces
111 Sibley Avenue, Second Floor
Ardmore, PA 19003
215-896-0860
Treacyfonts

Type Xpress
150 Fencl Lane
Hillside, IL 60162
708-982-6080
Fonts

UUU

U-Design Type Foundry
201 Ann Street
Hartford, CT 06103
203-278-3648
Barnhart Ornaments, Bill's Dingbats, Bill's Picture Fonts

Ultimate Technographics
4980 Buchan, #403
Montréal, QUE, Canada H4P 1S8
514-733-1188
Impostrip, MacImpostrip

U. S. MicroLabs
1611 Headway Circle, Building 3
Austin, TX 78754
512-339-0001
FontSizer

VVV

Ventura Software
15175 Innovation Drive
San Diego, CA 92128
619-673-7523
Xerox FormBase

VN Labs
4320 Campus Drive, #290
Newport Beach, CA 92660
714-474-6968
Diplomat Software Series Fonts

VS Software
PO Box 165920
Little Rock, AR 72216
501-376-2083
FontGen V, Font Library Manager, VS Fonts

WWW

Weaver Graphics
5165 South Highway A1A
Melbourne Beach, FL 32951
407-728-4000
LJFonts

Will-Harris Designer Disks
PO Box 480265
Los Angeles, CA 90048
Will-Harris Designer Disks

XYZ

Xitron
1428 East Ellsworth Road
Ann Arbor, MI 48108
313-971-8530
PM/CORA, VP/CORA

Zandar
8 Williston Street
Brattleboro, VT 05301
802-254-4244
TagWrite

Z-Soft
450 Franklin Road, #100
Marietta, GA 30067
404-428-0008
Publisher's Type Foundry, SoftType

Typographic Industry Terms and Conditions of Sale

Alterations, or AAs
Any additions or changes made by the customer to text, data, or style specifications originally submitted to the typographer. Also called Author's Alterations.

Alterations are not included in normal base rates and will be charged for additionally at rates prevailing at the time of the alteration. When type selection, sizes, and style are left to the best judgment of the typographer, any style changes are billable as customer alterations.

Charges for work
The basis upon which all work will be performed and billed.

Charges for work may be by job quotation, hourly rate, or unit price, at the discretion of the typographer, and will be billed as work is completed. Charges are considered accepted and due unless contested in writing within fifteen days of receipt of invoice.

Claims
Requests for price adjustments.

All claims of, or claims resulting from, defects, errors, shortages, or loss or damage of customer property must be made by customer in writing within thirty days of delivery of the respective part of an order, or it shall be considered irrevocably accepted.

Computer programs
A series of coded instructions or statements, designed to enable a computer to perform certain tasks.

Computer programs, system analyses, and related documentation developed for a customer are the property of the typographer. No use in whole or part shall be made of such programs or analyses without express permission and the payment of a mutually agreed upon compensation to the typographer.

Copy
The verbal, handwritten, typewritten, electronic, or printed words, data, or designs prepared for typesetting by the customer. Also called manuscript.

Copy or instructions that are incomplete, inaccurate, or poorly prepared will be accepted by the typographer at its discretion. Any costs incurred in making alterations to the work because of bad copy will be charged to the customer.

Corrections, or PEs
Changes in galleys, composition, or other work made necessary due to errors by the typographer.

Such errors will be corrected without charge when discovered on the next subsequent proof. Errors resulting from incomplete, inaccurate, or poorly prepared copy or data, or from handwritten or verbally submitted copy or changes, are considered billable alterations. No financial liability is assumed for errors beyond producing a corrected galley or page. (*Also see* Alterations.)

Customer's property
All manuscript, art work, media, materials, or supplies delivered to the typographer.

Customer's property is received and stored by the typographer without any liability for loss or damage from fire, water, theft, strikes, vandalism, Acts of God, or other causes beyond its control. The typographer's liability for computer tapes or disks is limited to replacement with blank media. All property used in producing work will be considered dead and disposable thirty days after completion of work unless subject to prior written agreement.

Delivery and shipping
Conveying of work to points or receivers designated by the customer.

All shipping and transportation charges are the responsibility of the customer. Delivery to a customer's designated representative, or to a common carrier, licensed trucker, or the Post Office shall constitute delivery and customer shall bear all risk of loss, delay, or damage thereafter. The typographer is not liable for any costs incurred as a result of late delivery, damage, or erroneous contents.

Electronic manuscript

Manuscript supplied by a customer on magnetic disk, or tape, or telecommunicated.

The typographer is not responsible for accidental damage to supplied media or for the accuracy of furnished input or final output. The typographer makes no representation of its ability to interface, read, or utilize disk input and assumes no liability therefor. Any additional translating, editing, or programming necessary to utilize customer-supplied files will be charged at prevailing rates.

Estimate

A nonbinding preliminary projection of charges or job cost.

Estimates are typically, but not exclusively, based on projections of the times and costs involved in performing a job based on customers' specifications, representations, and supplied sample copy and are not binding upon the typographer. (*Also see* Quotation.)

Experimental work

Attempts to create unique production tools, layouts, style sheets, dummies, or samples.

Experimental work, performed at the request of customers, shall be charged at the current prevailing rate.

Galley proofs

Preliminary reproductions of composition before being made up into page form.

See Preliminary Proofs.

Indemnification
Insurance and defense against third-party suits.

Customer agrees to indemnify the typographer against any expenses, costs, damages, or attorney's fees resulting from claims or suits of copyright infringement, libel, invasion of privacy, civil rights claims, or similar actions.

Input data
Information prepared for use on data-processing, word-processing, or typesetting computers.

Input and intermediate text and data produced by the typographer from paper or electronic manuscript remains the property of the typographer and may be destroyed upon completion of the work.

Layouts, style pages, and dummies
Preliminary or prototype versions of jobs, created as production tools.

Layouts, style sheets, dummies, or other special production tools required to be made by the typographer shall be charged for at prevailing rates. No use in whole or part shall be made of such production tools or prototypes without express permission and the payment of a mutually agreed upon compensation to the typographer.

Lien
The right to hold customer's property pending satisfaction of outstanding obligations.

All materials or property belonging to the customer, as well as work performed, may be retained as security until all just claims against the customer are satisfied.

Limitation of liability
Restrictions on typographer's liability that are considered in determining price.

Without prejudice to other clauses herein, the typographer's maximum liability, whether by negligence, contract, or otherwise, shall not exceed the return of the amount paid by customer for the work in dispute; and under no circumstances shall the typographer be liable for special, indirect, or consequential damages.

Media
The material on which computer codes and text are stored, including hard and floppy disks, magnetic tape, and paper tape.

All blank and recorded media supplied by the typographer, and all data, text, and codes stored thereon belong to the typographer and may be re-used or destroyed.

Metal
Type, rules, and spacing made from lead alloys.

All metal remains the property of the typographer, unless specifically purchased by customer.

Orders

Verbal or written requests for specific goods and/or services.

Acceptance of orders is subject to credit approval, and contingencies such as fire, water, strikes, theft, vandalism, Acts of God, and other causes beyond the typographer's control. Orders will be canceled only upon compensation for work already started and for related obligations.

Outside purchases

Materials purchased by the typographer to fulfill a customer's order.

All outside purchases will be charged for, based on cost and a markup for handling.

Overtime

Work performed by employees in excess of the regular schedule.

All required overtime is charged for additionally, at the typographer's prevailing rates for overtime.

Payment, late charges, title

Compensation for and ownership of work performed.

Payment is to be made in full within the period of the stated terms. Companies and individuals placing orders with a typographer are jointly and severally liable for payment for all work performed. Any amount not paid when due shall bear interest at the maximum prevailing state rate from the due date until paid. Title to all work remains with the typographer until all invoices and additional charges have been paid in full. If payment is not made within stated terms, customer shall be liable for all costs incurred in collection, including all attorney's fees and court costs.

Preliminary proofs

Reproductions of text, composition, and other graphic elements submitted for customer review. Also called customer, rough, galley, or reader proofs.

Proofs submitted to a customer for approval must be returned marked "OK" or "OK with Alterations or Corrections" (marked with standard proofreader's marks), dated, and initialed by the customer.

Quotation

A firm statement of price for which specified work will be performed, subject to credit approval.

Quotations will be given only if the actual manuscript is submitted in its entirety prior to the start of the job. Quotations are typically, but not exclusively, based on the nature and amount of copy, the condition of the manuscript or data, the style and other specifications, the job turnaround, and all delivery instructions originally submitted. Any change therefrom invalidates the quotation. Quotations are valid for thirty days unless otherwise stated, and must be in writing and be acknowledged by written purchase order. (*Also see* Estimate.)

Reader proofs

Preliminary reproductions of work to date submitted for customer review.

See Preliminary Proofs.

Reproduction proofs, or "repros"
Proofs of text, composition, and other graphic elements suitable for reproduction by photographic processes or offset lithography.

Reproduction proofs are intended to have a sharp reproducible image quality. They can be prepared in numerous acceptable manners and at any stage during the job.

Sample setting
Work produced for customer review in expectation of an order.

All sample type will be charged at the prevailing rate.

Standing type and mechanicals
Metal, film, or paper assembled for reproduction.

Type assembled for reproduction is considered dead seven days after use and may be disposed of without notice, unless subject to prior written agreement.

Taxes
Additional levy on work.

Unless otherwise stated, charges do not include taxes, and customer agrees to pay and be responsible for any sales, use, or other applicable tax, regardless of when liability for such tax is determined.

Telecommunications
Text or data transmitted over telephone lines from computer to computer or by facsimile reproduction of words on paper.

Customer shall pay for all transmission charges. Typographer is not responsible for any errors, omissions, or extra costs resulting from faults in the telephone network or from incompatibility between the sending and receiving computers.

Working negatives and positives
Photographic images on film or paper used in the production of work.

All intermediate photographic material made by or at the direction of the typographer remain the property of the typographer and may be disposed of without notice.

Index

AAs, defined, 179
Adobe, *see* PostScript; Adobe Type Manager
Aldus PageMaker, books on, 140–141
analog fonts, 20
Apple, System 7, 17
ASCII character set, 15
author's alterations, 179

BackLoader, 39
bar codes, 15, 78–79
Bézier curves, 16, 44
Bézier points, 18
bitmap font, 14
bitmap fonts, 28–30, 33–44
Bitstream, typography from, 17, 19

character sets, 14–16
charges, discussed, 179–180
chart designers, 77
claims, defined, 180
clipping path, 101
coding, 65
communications software, 88
computer programs, defined, 180
copy, defined, 180
copyfitting, software for, 75
corrections, 181
customer's property, discussed, 181

databases
    import filters for, 74–75
    publishing of, 89
DataShaper, 75

dbPublisher, 86
debugging, defined, 100
default font, 37
delivery, discussed, 181–182
design, books on, 136–139
desktop publishing, 5
    books on, 136–139
    as business, 7–8
    hardware for, 8
    software for, 8
display typefaces, 19
dot, defined, 22
download, defined, 14
downloaders, 37
drawing programs, 54
dummies, defined, 183–184

electronic manuscript, defined, 182
estimate, defined, 182
EUROASCII character set, 15
experimental work, defined, 182

family building, 37
field-delimited text, 75
fields, on forms, 86–87
file managers, 107–109
fixed spacing, 20
font cartridges, 15
Font/DA utility, 38
font editors
    features of, 48–49
    function of, 44

font editors *(continued)*
  multiple functions of, 45–46
  resolution of, 47
  software list, 50–51
font effects
  compared with drawing programs, 54
  convenience of, 54
  effectiveness of, 56
  software compatibility issues, 55–56
  software for, 56–58
  types of, 55
font family, 37
font format, 44, 46–47, 55
font format file, 20
font inventory, 37
font library, managing, 37–38
font metrics, 14, 16
font tables, 38
FONTastic Plus, 46
FontDisplay, 41
Fontographer, 48, 52
fonts
  Adobe, 17
  analog, 20
  Bézier control points, 18
  bitmap, 14, 28–30, 33–34
  compatibility with other software, 20
  data compressor for, 77
  default, 37
  defined, 13–14
  display, 19
  editing, 43–52
  effects used with, 53–58
  format of, 44, 46–47, 55
  future of, 23–24
  libraries of, 18
  for Macintosh, 24–30
  managing, 35–42
  for PC, 24–25, 30–34
  PCL, 30–33
  PostScript, 24–28
  and PostScript interpreters, 100–101
  printer, 14
  purchasing, 18
  resolution and, 21–23
  scalable, 14
  scaling, 78

scientific, 22
screen, 14, 36–37
service bureaus and, 19–20
software support, 18
specialty, 21
style sheet for, 42
vendors of, 17
format, font, 44, 46–47, 55
forms
  design of, 85–86
  field definition, 86–87
  filling, 86
  guidelines for, 84
  managing, 84–85, 87–88
  software for, 84–85
  software list for, 89–92
forms managers, 84–85, 87–88
  look-up feature, 88

galley proofs, defined, 183
Garth Graphic, 16
graphics tablets, 68–69

hard disk space, 15
hardware, 8
hyphenation, 72

IBM PCs and compatibles, *see* PCs
ICR systems, 80–81
imagesetters, 21–22
impact printers, 21
import filters, 49
  for database files, 74–75
  for word-processing files, 74
Impostrip, 73
indemnification, defined, 183
inferiors, defined, 44
Informed Designer, 85
Informed Mini-Manager, 85
innumeracy, explained, 47
input data, defined, 183
International Standards Organization (ISO), 14–15
ISO Latin 1 character set, 14–15

KernEdit, 60
kerning, 20
  databases for, 60–61

editing, 61
features of programs, 61–62
importance of, 59–60
screen display, 61
software list, 62–63
keyboard
layouts of, 38, 42
mapping and other considerations, 21
Kingsley/ATF, fonts from, 17

laser printer-to-plotter conversions, 75
laser printers, 21, 22–23
books on, 145–146
controller for, 77
late charges, discussed, 185–186
layouts, defined, 183–184
lien, defined, 184
ligatures, defined, 44
limitation of liability, 184
line, defined, 22
localized script managers, 21

Macintosh computers, 8
font editors for, 50–51
font effects for, 56–57
font managers for, 36–37
fonts for, 24–30
formware for, 89–90
kerning software for, 62–63
phototypesetting software, 97
PostScript interpreters for, 103–104
PostScript utilities for, 105
screen environments for, 40–41
template software for, 69
MacKern, 61
MathType, 52
mechanicals, defined, 187
media, defined, 184
metal, defined, 184
Metamorphosis, 52
MIDI interface, 72
Monotype, fonts from, 17
multilingual hyphenation, 72
music
typesetting for, 21
utilities for, 71–72

network support, 38

OCR-A and OCR-B character sets, 15
orders, defined, 185
outside purchases, discussed, 185
overtime, discussed, 185

payment, discussed, 185–186
PC computers, 8
font editors for, 48–49, 51
font effects for, 56, 57–58
font management for, 38
fonts for, 24–25, 30–34
formware for, 89, 90–92
import filters for, 49
interfacing with Apple, 108, 109
kerning software for, 62, 63
phototypesetting software, 97–98
PostScript interpreters for, 103–105
PostScript utilities for, 106
screen environments for, 41–42
template software for, 69, 70
PCL, 8
downloaders for, 38–39
font editors for, 51
formware for, 91–92
kerning packages for, 63
typography from, 17
PCL fonts, 30–33
periodicals on DTP, listed, 125–132
PEs, defined, 181
phototypesetting
drivers for, 93–96
graphics and, 94–95
on-line vs. off-line, 95–96
software for, 97–98
pixel, defined, 22
platforms, defined, 8
plotters, 75
PostScript, 8
books on, 144–145
development aids for, 102–103
editors for, 102–103
font editors for, 50–51
font effects for, 56–58
font managers and, 36

PostScript *(continued)*
   formware for, 89–91
   interpreters for, 99–106
   kerning packages for, 62–63
   phototypesetting software, 97–98
   printer upgrade boards for, 103–105
   template software for, 69–70
   utilities for, 105–106
PostScript fonts, 24–28
PostScript interpreters, software list, 103–105
pre-press assembly into signatures, 72–73
preliminary proofs, 186
price quotation, 186
printed communication, effective, 8–9
printer font, 14
printers
   laser, 75, 77, 145–146
   PostScript interpreters and, 101–102
   resolution of, 21–23
   upgrade boards for, 102, 103–105
production, 7
professional associations, listed, 121–124
programs, defined, 180
proofs, 183, 186–187
proportional spacing, 20
publication design, 6
Publisher's Type Foundry, 52
publishing
   commercial, 4
   desktop, 5
   noncommercial, 3–4
   production, 7

Quark XPress, books on, 144
quotation, defined, 186

reader proofs, 186
reproduction proofs, 187
repros, defined, 187
resolution
   font editor, 47
   phototypesetting, 96
   printer, 21–23
Roman 8 character set, 15

sample typesetting, discussed, 187
scalable font, 14
science, typesetting for, 21, 22
screen environments, 40
screen fonts, 14, 36–37
screen upgrades, 76
service bureaus, 19–20
   characteristics of, 113–115, 116–117
   defined, 111–112
   graphics and, 117
   problems of, 115–116
   terms and conditions of sale, 179–188
SGML, 66
shipping, discussed, 181–182
signatures, 73
software, 8
   buying, 10–11
spacing
   fixed, 20
   proportional, 20
spec sheet generation, software for, 76
specialty fonts, 21
specifications, 76
spline curves, 44
Standard Generalized Mark-up Language, 66
standing type, defined, 187
style sheet editors, 76–77
style sheets, discussed, 183–184
superiors, defined, 44

TAG command, 66
tagging, 65–66
taxes, defined, 87
telecommunications, 188
templates, 65–68
   graphics tablets, 68–69
   software list, 69–70
terminal emulation, 88
test files, 77
title, defined, 185–186
tracking, 20
transliteration, 21
TrueType, 15–16, 36
   fonts for, 17

TSRDownload, 39
tutorial software, 78
Type Manager, 15, 36–37, 45
typefaces, 16
   See also fonts
typesetting
   books on, 133–136
   conventional vs. DTP, 118
   drivers for, 93–96
   sample, 187
typography, books on, 133–136

upload, defined, 14
USASCII character set, 15
utilities, defined, 71

vector outlines, 44
vendors, list of, 147–177
Ventura 8 character set, 15
Ventura Publisher, 40
   books on, 141–143
videotex, 23
viruses, defined, 115
VTune, 40

word-processing files, import filters for, 74
working negatives and positives, 188
WYSIWYG, defined, 39

Xerox, *see* Ventura Publisher

zero-escapement characters, 21